KNITTING FROM THE CENTER OUT

An Introduction to Revolutionary Knitting with 28 Modern Projects

DANIEL YUHAS

Photography by Jody Rogac
Illustrations by Sun Young Park

STC Craft | A Melanie Falick Book

Stewart, Tabori & Chang, New York

FOR MY MOM

Published in 2012 by Stewart, Tabori & Chang
An imprint of ABRAMS

Text copyright © 2012 Daniel Yuhas
Illustrations copyright © 2012 Sun Young Park
Photographs copyright © Jody Rogac

Library of Congress Cataloging-in-Publication Data

Yuhas, Daniel.
  Knitting from the center out / Daniel Yuhas.
      pages cm
  STC Craft/A Melanie Falick Book.
  Includes bibliographical references and index.
  ISBN 978-1-58479-998-6 (alk. paper)
1. Knitting—Patterns. I. Title.
  TT825.Y84 2012
  746.43'2—dc23

                              2012001899

Editor: Melanie Falick
Book Design: Anna Christian
Creative Direction/Photography: Karen Schaupeter
Production Manager: Tina Cameron

The text of this book was composed in Router and Shinn.

Printed and bound in China.

10 9 8 7 6 5 4 3 2 1

Stewart, Tabori & Chang books are available at special discounts when purchased
in quantity for premiums and promotions as well as fundraising or educational
use. Special editions can also be created to specification. For details, contact
specialsales@abramsbooks.com or the address below.

THE ART OF BOOKS SINCE 1949
115 West 18th Street
New York, NY 10011
www.abramsbooks.com

CONTENTS

INTRODUCTION

I learned to knit as a gender-bending kid in college. I was at Oberlin College in Ohio in the early 1990s, where "Subvert the Dominant Paradigm" was so much the motto of the day that someone on campus decided to subvert *that* by graffiti-ing "Subdominate the Pervertadigm" everywhere. Oberlin was teeming with eighteen-year-old gender-benders like me, so the sight of a male student knitting was no big shakes—we had clothing-optional dinners and coed dorm rooms after all!

But what had started out in part as an ironic gesture soon became an obsession. I took to knitting right away in part because of the feeling of freedom it gave me—there is no wrong way to knit. I found endless inspiration in the stitch dictionary at the back of the *Vogue Knitting Encyclopedia*, and a supply of unraveled thrift-store sweaters gave me all the yarn I needed to play with. From the very beginning, I was fascinated by learning knitting's rules. Then, in the tradition of many knitters before me, my first impulse was usually to bend or break them to see what would happen. Many of my early experiments ended up as tangled blobs that I later unraveled, but the keepers became one-of-a-kind garments for my friends and family.

Years later, when my youngest sister was pregnant, I decided to knit a blanket for the new baby. I found a pattern book at the library, and one design in particular called to me—the blanket was made of lacy octagonal stars, pieced together with squares between them like a quilt. The technique was brand new to me. The octagons in the blanket were worked outward from the center on double-pointed needles, starting with only eight stitches and adding more with every round. It was a tricky technique to learn, especially at the start when there were only a couple of stitches on each needle. Once I got the hang of it, though, I was hooked. Knitting this way had a pleasant logic to it, and I discovered that it was easy to find my place if I lost track, by counting stitches and reading my knitting.

I was soon knitting one octagon after another on autopilot, and ended up making a blanket larger than the pattern had called for—I just got carried away!

The next time someone I loved was expecting, I continued the tradition. This time I improvised a design of my own. Starting with the octagon shape I had learned from that first blanket and adding more and more increases, I created a piece that grew rufflier and rufflier toward the edges. In the odd way that inspiration works, my experience making an eight-sided blanket started me thinking about knitting an eight-legged creature, and the next thing I knew the blanket was done and I was knitting the prototype for an octopus. That second blanket and the octopus (a version of which is included here on page 73) were also the first two patterns I published online.

My creative practice has often been to pose a question, then see what happens when I try to answer it on the needles. And like the blanket inspiring the octopus, one question often leads to another. As I started experimenting with the center-out method of knitting, I tapped into a fascinating series of questions. What shapes could I make? What would happen if I increased and decreased in the same round? What if I combined center-out knitting with textured stitch patterns, or lace? Each design idea contained within it the germ of the next, and I grew as a designer as I explored each one. My head was spinning with the possibilities.

I found center-out knitting both fast and addictive. Since it begins with just a few stitches, the early stages of each project progress by leaps and bounds, which is great when you're making something like a baby blanket with a due date for a deadline. And since it's usually not necessary to stop and turn the work around, I find it that much harder to put my work down without knitting "just one more round." Even in making larger pieces, the stitch pattern evolves as the work grows. One round is seldom the same as the last, keeping things lively.

Starting in the middle gives center-out knitting a built-in roundness and symmetry. Varying this pattern in surprisingly simple ways produces beautiful shapes: I designed shawls and blankets for this book in the shape of flowers, stars, spirals, and polygons.

Starting in the center also makes gauge far less important. For example, you can knit a well-fitting hat without stopping to swatch first by starting at the top and working outward, and continuing to knit until it fits. You'll find a pattern to make your own Swatchless Watch Cap on page 40. Similarly, many of the projects in this book can be made to different dimensions or knit with yarn of varying weights without changing the pattern at all—just keep going until you've made the size you want. The Cone Hat (page 33), Sunflower Shawl (page 96), and Tree of Life Afghan (page 119) are all adaptable in this way.

So what do I mean by calling this book an introduction to "revolutionary knitting"? I certainly don't mean to imply that revolutionary knitting is brand new—I often call it a "revolutionary old technique." The Medallion Cap on page 45 was directly inspired by antique bonnet caps dating as far back as the early eighteenth century, and I discovered an antique version of the octagonal blanket that kicked off my own obsession. In the nineteenth century, knitters in the Azores islands in the North Atlantic produced astonishing center-out lace work. And twentieth-century masters like Herbert Niebling and Marianne Kinzel pushed the art of knitted lace even further.

I mean "revolutionary knitting" literally: Each spin around the needles is one revolution, so center-out knitting is, quite simply, revolutionary. But I also mean it metaphorically: I created each project in this book with the excitement of a new discovery, a miniature creative revolution, and I want to share that head-spinning feeling of wonder, possibility, and fun with you. I hope you will become as excited as I am about the surprising shapes your knitting will take.

In Chapter 1, I present an overview of the shapes that are the building blocks of center-out knitting and how they are formed. You'll find these basic shapes repeated over and over throughout the pieces I designed for this book. Then in Chapters 2–6, I present a collection of my favorite projects, from a simple I-cord necklace to a lace shawl in the shape of a sunflower. With accessories, hats, socks, mittens, blankets, shawls, toys, and sweaters included, you can see that revolutionary knitting is a versatile technique. I made sure in choosing these designs that each project takes a slightly different spin on the revolutionary knitting technique, so there's something new to learn in each one.

Starting on page 143, you'll find illustrated, step-by-step tutorials for the few techniques you'll need to know in order to knit from the center out. There you'll find your choice of three cast-on methods that work well with revolutionary knitting, as well as instructions on the most common ways of knitting from the center out: working with double-pointed needles, the Magic Loop Method, or two circular needles. Whether you're brand new to these techniques or need a refresher, I hope you'll find this a valuable resource.

As much as I love seeing people knit my designs, I find it even more thrilling when someone adapts what I've done and makes something truly their own, or simply uses an idea I shared as a starting point to come up with something completely different. Once you've knitted a few projects to get the hang of the center-out technique, I feel sure that you will be able to design your own pieces. You may be able to create a revolution of your own. I hope so!

MAGIC NUMBERS
and the rhythm of center-out knitting

Center-out, or revolutionary, knitting starts in the middle and grows outward. And unlike most knitting in the round, which starts by casting on a large circle of stitches, center-out knitting is usually begun by casting on a few stitches and joining them into a circle. Every turn around that circle makes up one round, and each round ends back where it started, but one row higher. Center-out knitting is shaped as the work revolves around and around that circle, creating new stitches by working increases so that the knitting grows wider as it grows outward from the center. The number of increases we put into each round determines the shape our project takes. Like magic! Once you understand the underlying logic and rhythm, the possibilities are endless.

MAKING I-CORD

To make I-cord, begin by casting a few stitches onto a double-pointed or circular needle. Knit a row and then, instead of turning and purling back the way you came, slide the stitches back to the working end of the needle without turning around. Draw the working yarn behind the stitches from left to right, and knit them again. Repeat this process and your work will form a quickly growing tube. Each round of I-cord climbs up on top of the last one, like knitting your way up a spiral staircase.

TUBES (no increases at all)

If we cast on a few inches' worth of stitches and join our work into a circle, then start working around without increasing or decreasing, the knitting will form a tube, like the cuff of a sock or the trunk of a sweater. If we cast on only a few stitches and work those in the round, we'll get a skinny tube called I-cord (see left). The first section of projects in this book features designs that use I-cord, whether as a border element, as in the Lace and Loop Scarf (page 22), or the main fabric of the piece, like the Coral Necklace (page 17). You'll also find I-cord used as a beginning to some of the hats, like the Medallion Caps (page 45), since a few rounds of I-cord are an easy and attractive way to begin a piece of revolutionary knitting.

CONES (increase 1 stitch per round)

If we increase at a rate of about one stitch per round, our knitting will form a cone. The Cone Hat (page 33), Sorting Hat (page 36), and Foxglove Boa (page 26) projects in this book all use this shape.

CIRCLES AND POLYGONS
(increase 4 stitches per round)

In the same way that you can use the number π in geometry to figure out the area of a circle, 4 is the magic number for creating revolutionary knitting that will lie flat. In almost all cases, increasing at a rate of 4 stitches per round will produce flat fabric. However, this usually doesn't mean that 4 stitches are added in each round; you might work a round without increases, then double up the increases on the following round. For example, in the pinwheel blanket discussed on page 12, 8 stitches are increased every other round.

Many of the possibilities for creating flat, center-out fabric are explored in Chapter 5: Shawls + Blankets.

DOMES (increase 3½ stitches per round)

Increasing at a rate slightly less than 4 stitches per round will produce fabric that's almost flat, but not quite. For example, dividing the work into 7 sections and increasing by 7 stitches every other round gives us an increase rate of 3½ stitches per round. This is a great technique for making the top of a hat, as I've done in the Medallion Caps (page 45) and the Swatchless Watch Cap (page 40).

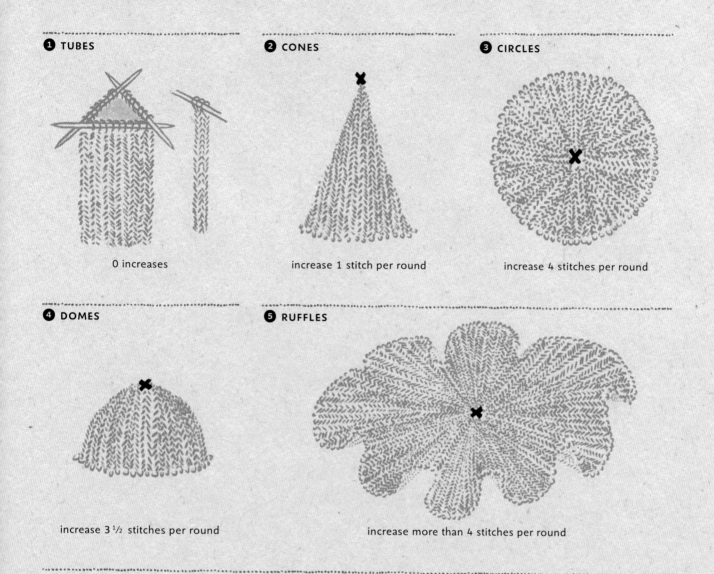

❶ TUBES

0 increases

❷ CONES

increase 1 stitch per round

❸ CIRCLES

increase 4 stitches per round

❹ DOMES

increase 3 ½ stitches per round

❺ RUFFLES

increase more than 4 stitches per round

RUFFLES (increase more than 4 stitches per round)

Knowing that increasing at a rate of 4 stitches per round will give us flat fabric, what happens if we increase by more than 4 stitches per round? For example, what if we increase into every stitch, so that each round has twice as many stitches as the last? Each of our increases widens the fabric by one stitch, but the height doesn't grow fast enough to accommodate the new fabric. The result is a ruffle. The greater the number of stitches we produce in each round, the rufflier the fabric will be. The Foxglove Boa (page 26) and Feather and Fan Shawl (page 111) projects both use ruffles as their edging.

THE RHYTHM OF REVOLUTIONARY KNITTING

The traditional pinwheel blanket is one of the simplest and most popular center-out projects. The instructions are quick and easy to remember because of their logic and natural rhythm. "Cast on 8 stitches and join into a round. Divide into 8 sections. *Knit, increasing at the start of each section every other round. Repeat from *."

Or, in other words: Begin by casting on 8 stitches. Arrange the stitches into a circle, and place markers to divide the work into 8 equal sections. In the first round, knit all of the stitches. In the second round, increase into the first stitch of each section while knitting the rest. In the pinwheel blanket shown at right, I knit into the front and back of the first stitch of each section to make my increases. Eight new stitches are added every other round, so the pinwheel contains 8, then 16, 24, and 32 stitches, and so on. The blanket grows wider and taller with each spin around the needles, and the knitting takes on an octagonal (eight-sided) shape. Logical, right?

To demonstrate how the rhythm of revolutionary knitting changes as the work grows larger, take a close look at the concentric circles on the blanket shown here. I made each ring of color using only 20 yards of yarn, so each one has approximately the same number of stitches and took about the same time to make. You can see how each section of color is thinner and farther around than the last as the project grows bigger. Similarly, the beginning of each project will progress quickly, then the pace will gradually slow down as the knitting progresses.

PUTTING IT ALL TOGETHER

Most of the projects in this book are made by combining a few of the building blocks outlined on pages 10–11 into the design. For example, the Sorting Hat (page 36) is begun as a cone, then finished with a large, circular brim. In the Foxglove Boa (page 26), what begins as a tube of I-cord branches out into several cones, then each cone ends with a ruffle. And although they're very different projects, you'll find the same basic shaping in the Geometric Shrug (page 128) as the Half-Moon Mittens (page 49). Once you understand these basic shapes, you may find yourself combining them in your knitting in interesting and unexpected ways. I'd love to see what you come up with.

1 TUBES

2 CONES

3 CIRCLES

4 DOMES

5 RUFFLES

6 PUTTING IT ALL TOGETHER

I-CORD WONDERS

If we knit just a few stitches in a circle, the result would be a skinny knitted tube. Knitting guru Elizabeth Zimmermann accidentally figured out a way to make this tube by using two double-pointed needles and dubbed her discovery "Idiot Cord," or I-cord for short. I-cord is the simplest form of circular knitting, and an easy way to begin revolutionary knitting. Drawing the yarn behind the work joins the stitches into a round in one easy move. Each of the projects in this section explores the possibilities of I-cord in a different way, whether it's used as the main fabric of the piece, as in the Coral Necklace, or as a decorative edging, as in the Lace and Loop Scarf.

coral necklace

This twisted necklace may look like one extremely long length of I-cord, but it has a trick to it. You begin with a few rows of flat, back-and-forth knitting, then divide the work into seven equal sections. Each of these sections is worked in I-cord to form one necklace strand. After all seven strands are complete, the strands are transferred back to a single needle and knit across, rejoining the work. You then give the bottom end a couple of twists before grafting to the opposite end, permanently setting the necklace's twist.

STITCH PATTERNS

Twisted Stockinette Stitch
Knit all sts through the back loop on RS rows, purl all sts through the back loop on WS rows. *Note: WS rows are worked only when working the gauge swatch.*

Stripe Pattern
Working in Twisted St st, *work 1 rnd in A, then 1 rnd in B; repeat from * for Stripe Pattern.

STARTING NECKLACE

Using waste yarn, CO 35 sts. Change to A and Twisted St st. Work even for 1 row; do not turn. Slide sts to opposite end of needle. Change to B; work even in Twisted St st for 1 row; do not turn. Transfer first 30 sts to st holder. Slide remaining 5 sts back to opposite end of needle.

WORKING I-CORD STRANDS

Note: When changing colors, do not break yarn; simply let old color hang at end of rnd, then pick up new color from underneath old color to avoid twisting yarns. Break yarns only when each Strand is complete.

Working on 5 remaining sts only, work I-cord (see page 10) in Stripe Pattern until I-cord Strand measures 28" from the beginning, ending with a rnd in B. Break yarns and transfer sts to second st holder. *Transfer next 5 sts from left-hand end of first st holder to dpn. Rejoin A and work as for first I-cord Strand. Repeat from * until 7 I-cord Strands have been worked, leaving last I-cord Strand on needle.

FINISHED MEASUREMENTS
29" circumference

YARN
The Fibre Company Organik (70% organic merino / 15% baby alpaca / 15% silk; 98 yards / 50 grams) 1 hank each Magma (A) and Coral Reef (B)

NEEDLES
One pair double-pointed needles (dpn) size US 6 (4 mm)

Change needle size if necessary to obtain correct gauge.

NOTIONS
Waste yarn; stitch holders

GAUGE
24 sts and 28 rows = 4" (10 cm) in Twisted Stockinette Stitch (St st)
Note: Gauge not critical for this project.

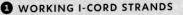

① WORKING I-CORD STRANDS

5 stitches each strand

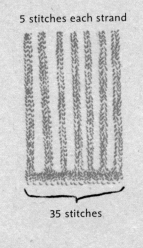

35 stitches

② FINISHING

35 stitches

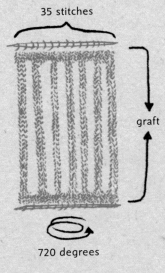

graft

720 degrees

FINISHING

Transfer live I-cord sts back to same needle, being careful not to twist I-cord Strands. Slide sts to right-hand end of needle. Join A and work 1 row in Twisted St st. Break yarn.

Carefully unravel waste yarn and place live sts on second dpn. Rotate second dpn 2 full times (720 degrees) so that I-cord Strands are now twisted. Using B and Kitchener st (see page 154), graft live sts, making sure that you graft RS to RS.

Block as desired.

VARIATIONS

I-cord is an easy and fun technique for experimentation. You may want to try varying this pattern by changing the length, width, or number of I-cord strands or trying different stitch textures or color combinations. You could also experiment with adding extra twists in the finishing, intentionally twisting the individual columns, or leaving the strands untwisted. Remember that variations will also affect the yarn requirements.

pearls

A knitted tube expands and contracts to form these silken pearls. To make them, work a short length of I-cord, then increase until the cord becomes a half-dome. Next stuff the half-dome with a cotton ball, then decrease back to the I-cord.

PEARLS

Using waste yarn, CO 5 sts. Join to work in the rnd, being careful not to twist sts.

Rnds 1–3: Work I-cord (see page 10). Divide stitches between 2 or more needles if necessary for your preferred method of working in the rnd.

Rnds 5, 7, 9–11, 13, and 15: Knit.

Rnd 4: *M1, k1; repeat from * to end—10 sts.

Rnd 6: *M1, k2; repeat from * to end—15 sts.

Rnd 8: *M1, k3; repeat from * to end—20 sts.

Rnd 12: *K2, k2tog; repeat from * to end—15 sts remain. Stuff Pearl with cotton ball.

Rnd 14: *K1, k2tog; repeat from * to end—10 sts remain.

Rnd 16: *K2tog; repeat from * to end—5 sts remain. Slip all sts to 1 needle.

Repeat Rnds 1–16 until you have made 15 Pearls.

FINISHING

Carefully unravel waste yarn and place live sts on second dpn or opposite end of circ needle. Using Kitchener st (see page 154), graft live sts, making sure that you graft RS to RS.

VARIATIONS

To make a longer or shorter necklace, separate the Pearls with longer or shorter sections of I-cord. To create Pearls of varying sizes, modify the increase pattern. If substituting yarn, work at a tight gauge so the cotton ball won't show through. Remember that variations will also affect the yarn requirements.

FINISHED MEASUREMENTS

Pearls: Approximately 3 ½" circumference

Necklace: Approximately 27" long

YARN

Shibui Knits Heichi (100% silk; 105 yards / 50 grams): 1 hank Column

NEEDLES

Two 16" (40 cm) long or longer circular (circ) needles or one set of three double-pointed needles (dpn), size US 4 (3.5 mm). *Note: Because this project is worked at a tight gauge using a yarn with very little bounce, I recommend using metal needles.*

Change needle size if necessary to obtain correct gauge.

NOTIONS

Waste yarn; 15 jumbo cotton balls; stitch marker

GAUGE

22 sts and 28 rows = 4" (10 cm) in Stockinette Stitch (St st)

start here

I-cord

increase

decrease

stuff with cottonball

lace and loop scarf

FINISHED MEASUREMENTS
6" wide at narrowest point, not including loops

26" wide at widest point x 60" long

YARN
Louet Euroflax Sport Weight (100% wet spun linen; 270 yards / 100 grams): 2 hanks #42 Eggplant

NEEDLES
One pair straight needles size US 7 (4.5 mm)

One pair double-pointed needles (dpn) size US 7 (4.5 mm)

Change needle size if necessary to obtain correct gauge.

GAUGE
15 sts and 22 rows = 4" (10 cm) in Stockinette stitch (St st)

In other designs in this book, I used I-cord on its own, as the beginning of a piece of center-out knitting, or to make a smooth tubular edging. In designing this scarf, I wanted to push the possibilities of I-cord a little bit further. What would happen, I wondered, if I worked across a row of flat knitting, then stopped and made a tube of I-cord? I daydreamed about roller coasters as I followed the I-cord through twists and turns, and came up with this looped edging for my lacy scarf.

To begin this scarf, you work back and forth in an easy lace pattern on straight needles. Then, every sixth row, nine stitches before the end of the row, you work a four-stitch tube of I-cord on two spare double-pointed needles. That tube does a somersault to form a loop that wraps around the remaining fabric before you resume the back-and-forth knitting to finish the row. Each loop is locked into place without any sewing, by simply purling back across the next row.

SCARF
Using straight needles, CO 29 sts. Purl 1 row.

Looped Section
Rows 1 and 3: K2tog, *yo, k2tog; repeat from * to last 9 sts, k8, yo, k1.

Rows 2 and 4: Purl.

Row 5: K2tog, *yo, k2tog; repeat from * to last 9 sts, slip next 4 sts to dpn. With second dpn, work these 4 sts in I-cord (see page 10) for 30 rnds. Pass dpn down away from you, then bring it forward and around the left side of the Scarf to form a Loop. The live sts at the top of the completed Loop will be in the same position relative to the two straight needles as when the Loop began. Be careful not to twist the I-cord when forming the Loop. Transfer live sts from the completed Loop back to right-hand straight needle, k4, yo, k1 from left-hand needle (see illustration, page 24). *Note: If you use a circ instead of straight needles, it will be necessary to pass the ball of yarn together with the I-cord loop to avoid tangling the working yarn in the cable of the circ.*

Row 6: Purl.

Repeat Rows 1–6 until you have completed 25 loops.

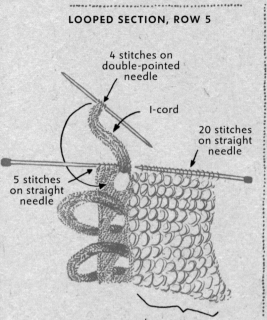

LOOPED SECTION, ROW 5

4 stitches on double-pointed needle

I-cord

20 stitches on straight needle

5 stitches on straight needle

lace pattern

Straight Section

Row 1: *K2tog, yo; repeat from * to last st, k1.

Row 2: Purl.

Repeat Rows 1 and 2 until piece measures 12" from last completed loop, ending with Row 2.

Expanding Lace

Row 1: K2, *yo, k2tog, repeat from * to last st, yo, k1—30 sts.

Row 2: Purl.

Row 3: K1, *yo, k2tog, repeat from * to last st, yo, k1—31 sts.

Row 4: Purl.

Repeat Rows 1–4, increasing 1 st every other row, until piece measures 60" from the beginning, ending with Row 2 or 4. You should have approximately 76 sts.

Ruffled Edge

Row 1: K1, *yo, k1; repeat from * to end.

Row 2: Purl.

Bind off all sts knitwise.

FINISHING

Block as desired.

VARIATIONS

You may wish to make your Scarf longer or shorter, or vary the length or width of the I-cord loops. If substituting yarn, know that different fibers will behave quite differently. For example, a springy animal-fiber yarn such as merino wool will create bouncy loops but be more prone to curling. Remember that variations will also affect the yarn requirements.

FINISHED MEASUREMENTS

Boa: Approximately 32" long

Flowers: Approximately 4" long x 3½" circumference, not including Ruffle

YARN

Blue Sky Alpacas Suri Merino (60% baby suri alpaca / 40% merino wool; 164 yards / 100 grams): 3 hanks #424 Wildfire

NEEDLES

One set of four or five double-pointed needles (dpn) size US 5 (3.75 mm), or one or two 36" (90 cm) long or longer circular (circ) needle(s) size US 5 (3.75 mm).

Change needle size if necessary to obtain correct gauge.

NOTIONS

Stitch markers; 25 safety pins; 25 pieces of card stock or heavy paper 6 x 6" square; liquid spray starch (optional)

GAUGE

22 sts and 32 rows = 4" (10 cm) in Stockinette Stitch (St st). *Note: Gauge is not essential for this project.*

foxglove boa

This "boa" was inspired by the natural shapes of flowers, like a stalk of foxgloves or a vine of morning glories climbing a fence. Instead of beginning at the center, you work the first flower from the outside in, decreasing until you have only 5 stitches left. These 5 stitches are worked as an I-cord tube to create the stem. Every few rounds, you make a branch in the stem by working increases, then set the newly minted stitches aside on a safety pin, saving them to be worked once the stem is complete. Then, one by one, you remove the pins, rejoin the yarn, and add a flower to each branch.

Each flower is worked as a cone by increasing one stitch every round. You form the edge of each flower by knitting into the front and back of each stitch, doubling the number of stitches. The more stitches you add, the rufflier the fabric becomes, so each conical flower ends with an energetic and bouncy edge.

I-CORD STEM

Bottom Flower

CO 96 sts. Divide sts among 2 or more needles if necessary for your preferred method of working in the rnd. Join for working in the rnd, being careful not to twist sts; pm for beginning of rnd.

Rnds 1 and 3: Knit.

Rnds 2 and 4: *K2tog; repeat from * to end—24 sts remain after Rnd 4. Remove beginning-of-rnd marker.

Divide work into 3 sections (8 sts per section), either by placing markers or by dividing sts among 3 dpns, with 1 section per dpn.

Next Rnd: *K2tog, knit to end of section, knit all sts for next 3 sections (1 st decreased each rnd); repeat from * until 5 sts remain. *Note: On each rnd, you will work the first needle in the rnd twice, thereby moving the beginning of the rnd section ahead with every rnd.*

Remove markers.

BRANCHES

Note: Each set of 3 held sts constitutes one Branch. Each Branch will be set aside for its Flower to be worked after the Stem is complete. You may use safety pins to hold the sts.

Rnds 1–3: *Work 5-st I-cord (see page 10).

Rnd 4: [K1-f/b] 3 times, k2—8 sts.

Rnd 5: Knit. Transfer sts 1, 2, and 3 to a safety pin.

Rnds 6–9: Repeat Rnds 1–4.

Rnd 10: Knit. Transfer sts 2, 3, and 4 to a safety pin.

Rnds 11–13: Repeat Rnds 1–3.

Rnd 14: K2, [k1-f/b] 3 times—8 sts.

Rnd 15: Knit. Transfer sts 3, 4, and 5 to a safety pin.

Rnds 16–19: Repeat Rnds 11–14.

Rnd 20: Knit. Transfer sts 4, 5, and 6 to a safety pin.

Rnds 21–24: Repeat Rnds 11–14.

Rnd 25: Knit. Transfer sts 5, 6, and 7 to a safety pin.

Repeat Rnds 1–25 until you have 25 Branches.

FLOWERS

Top Flower

Cone
Rnd 1: Slide sts back to right-hand end of needle. K1-f/b, knit to end—6 sts. Divide work into 3 sections (2 sts each section), either by placing markers or by dividing sts among 3 dpns, with 1 section per dpn.

Rnd 2: *K1-f/b, knit to end of section; knit all sts for next 3 sections (1 st increased each rnd); repeat from

* until you have 24 sts (8 sts each section). *Note: On each repeat, you will work the first section in the rnd twice, thereby moving the beginning of the rnd 1 section ahead with every rnd.*

Ruffle
Rnds 1 and 3: *K1-f/b; repeat from * to end—96 sts after Rnd 3.

Rnds 2 and 4: Purl.

BO all sts knitwise.

Remaining Flowers
Rnd 1: With RS facing, transfer 3 sts from Branch safety pin to dpn; rejoin yarn. Knit; do not turn.

Rnd 2: Slide sts back to right-hand end of needle. *K1-f/b; repeat from * to end—6 sts.

Complete as for Top Flower, beginning with Rnd 2.

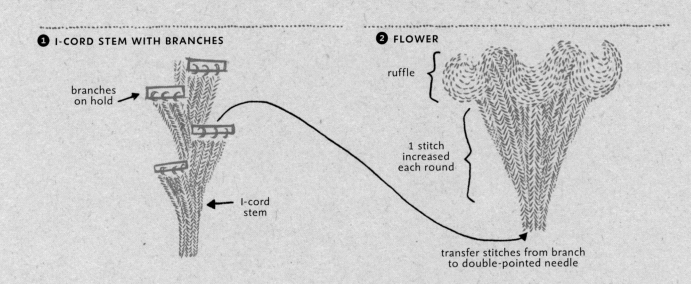

❶ I-CORD STEM WITH BRANCHES

branches on hold →

← I-cord stem

❷ FLOWER

ruffle {

1 stitch increased each round

transfer stitches from branch to double-pointed needle

FINISHING

Cut 25 pieces of heavy paper or cardstock into 6 x 6" squares. Roll around one corner into a cone shape that conforms to shape of Flower; tape edges together. Paper cone should be at least 1" longer than Flower. Cut paper cone as needed so it will stand with pointed end upwards. Make 24 more cones identical to the first. Soak Boa and place one Flower over each paper cone. Allow to air dry. To help Flowers hold their body, you may spray the insides with liquid starch (optional).

VARIATIONS

This pattern will work as written with yarn of many different gauges. If substituting yarn, use a needle one or two sizes smaller than the yarn manufacturer recommends, to achieve a tight stitch. You may wish to make flowers larger or smaller than shown here, or experiment with using different combinations of colors and yarns. A multicolored boa would make a great stash-busting project for using up leftover yarn.

TUBE + CONE + RUFFLE = FLOWER
magic numbers in action

The Foxglove Boa design combines three of the building blocks of revolutionary knitting. The stem is worked as a skinny tube of I-cord. Increases in sets of three are made in the tube to form the branches, but the new stitches made by those increases are set aside on safety pins as soon as they are worked, so the overall increase rate for the stem is zero. After you rejoin the yarn to each branch, each flower begins in the shape of a cone, made by increasing one stitch per round. Each flower ends with a ruffle. To form the ruffle, instead of increasing by the same number of stitches in each increase round, you double the stitch count by knitting into the front and back of every stitch. So you have 24 stitches before the ruffle starts, then 48, then 96. You could experiment by repeating this increase round a few more times, giving you 192, then 384 stitches. The ruffliness of the fabric would become more and more energetic with each trip around the needles. But be warned— ten rounds like this and you'd have 12,288 stitches!

HATS + MITTENS + SOCKS

The projects in this chapter are all about using center-out knitting to create well-fitting, good-looking accessories. This is a perfect application for center-out knitting, which so naturally forms rounded shapes that easily stretch around our heads, hands, and feet. The hats are worked downward from the top until they reach the desired size—the simplest example of just "knitting until it fits." The socks and mittens are worked in some innovative ways. One pair of socks is worked upward from the toe; another pair begins under the ball of the heel. And the mittens are worked in one piece in a surprising series of maneuvers, beginning at the tip of the thumb and ending at the cuff.

cone hats

These playful dress-up hats explore the limits of gravity-defying knitting. Beginning at the tip and increasing by only one stitch per round, the cone takes on a very pointy tapered shape. Working at a very tight gauge contributes to the stay-put nature of the fabric.

STITCH PATTERN

1x1 Rib (even number of sts; 1-rnd repeat)
All Rnds: *K1, p1; repeat from * to end.

SPECIAL TECHNIQUE

Tubular BO (optional)
Setup Rnd: *K1, slip 1 wyif; repeat from * to end. Holding 2 needles parallel to each other, *slip 1 knit st onto front needle and 1 slipped st onto back needle; repeat from * until all sts are divided. *Note: You may find it easier to spread sts out over 4 needles—2 for knit sts and 2 for slipped sts.* Using Kitchener st (see page 154), graft sts on front needle to sts on back needle.

HAT

Using Backward Loop CO (see page 154), color of your choice, and tail of yarn, CO 3 sts. Begin I-cord (see page 10); work even for 3 rnds. Divide sts among 2 or more needles if necessary for your preferred method of working in the rnd; do not pm for beginning of rnd.

Shape Hat

Note: Each rnd will end 2 sts to the left of where it began.

Rnd 1: RLI, k5—4 sts.

Rnd 2: RLI, k6—5 sts.

Rnd 3: RLI, k7—6 sts.

Rnd 4: RLI, k8—7 sts.

Rnd 5: RLI, k9—8 sts.

Rnd 6: RLI, k10—9 sts.

Rnd 7: RLI, k11—10 sts

SIZES

Toddler (Child, Woman, Man)

FINISHED MEASUREMENTS

13 ½ (15, 16 ¾, 18 ¼)" circumference
Approximately 11 ½ (12 ¾, 14, 15 ¼)" tall

YARN

Morehouse Merinos 3-Strand Worsted Weight (100% merino wool; 140 yards / 2 ounces); **Solid Color Version:** 1 (1, 1, 2) hank(s) Geranium; **Two-Color Version:** 1 (1, 1, 2) hank(s) Quail; 1 hank Geranium. *Note: Hat is worked at a tighter gauge than yarn calls for so that the point will stand up straight.*

NEEDLES

One set of four or five double-pointed needles (dpn) size US 3 (3.25 mm), or one or two 36" (90 cm) long or longer circular (circ) needle(s), size US 3 (3.25 mm)

Change needle size if necessary to obtain correct gauge.

NOTIONS

Eight stitch markers (1 in color A, 7 in color B)

GAUGE

22 sts and 33 rows = 4" (10 cm) in Stockinette stitch (St st)

1 HAT SHAPING

Start here and increase 1 stitch per round.

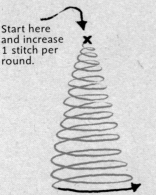

2 FINISHED HAT

Rnd 8: RLI, k12—11 sts.

Rnd 9: RLI, k13—12 sts.

Rnd 10: RLI, k14—13 sts.

Rnd 11: RLI, k15—14 sts. Place marker (color A) for beginning of rnd and place 7 additional markers (color B) to divide work into 7 sections of 2 sts each. You will have markers A and B together at beginning of rnd.

Next Rnd: RLI, knit to marker A, remove marker A, leaving marker B in place, knit to next marker B, reposition marker A for new beginning of rnd—15 sts.

Note: The piece is divided into 7 sections, but on each rnd, after you work the increase, you will work 8 sections, then reposition the beginning of rnd marker, thereby moving the beginning of rnd 1 section ahead with every rnd.

Continue as established, increasing 1 st at the beginning of the rnd, working through beginning of rnd to next marker, and repositioning marker A to mark new beginning of rnd, until you have 75 (84, 93, 102) sts. If you are using a different weight yarn, continue working increases until piece measures 13 ½ (15, 16 ¾, 18 ¼)" in circumference, ending with an even number of sts; piece should measure approximately 10 (11 ¼, 12 ½, 13 ¾)" from tip. For Two-Color Version, change to contrasting color; knit 1 rnd.

Next Rnd: Change to 1x1 Rib; work even until ribbing measures 1 ½". Bind off all sts in pattern, or use Tubular BO for a smooth bottom edge.

VARIATIONS

For an alternative construction that will wow your knitting friends, instead of dividing the work with markers, try distributing the stitches among seven double-pointed needles. Use a dissimilar needle (for example, metal or plastic instead of bamboo) as the working needle in the first round. Each increase section will be worked with the dissimilar needle.

This pattern will work as written with many different weight yarns. Simply work as instructed until you get to the correct circumference for your size. Depending on your gauge, your hat may be slightly more or less pointy than pictured here. If substituting yarn, be sure to use needles a few sizes smaller than what the manufacturer recommends for their yarn in order to achieve a tighter gauge than is recommended; this will ensure that the fabric is stiff enough for the hat to stand up straight. Remember that variations will also affect the yarn requirements.

sorting hat

A bumpy, textured stitch and a blooming, mohair-infused woolen yarn combine to create the "witchy" fabric of this hat. When I tried this on during an early show-and-tell meeting with my editor, it reminded us of the Sorting Hat in the Harry Potter novels.

The random-looking zigzag texture in this hat is formed by repeating a simple knit-and-purl stitch pattern while, at the same time, increasing one stitch in every round. After your hat grows large enough to accommodate the wearer's head, you work a wide brim in garter stitch, increasing every fourth round to create a flat circle of fabric. A loop of pipe cleaners or beading wire is worked into the I-cord bind-off to hold the edge of the brim in place.

SIZES
Child (Adult Small, Adult Large)

FINISHED MEASUREMENTS
16 (18, 20)" circumference. *Note: Hat will stretch to fit head 2" larger than finished circumference.*

Approximately 13 (14 ½, 16)" tall with 14 (14, 16)" diameter Brim

YARN
Green Mountain Spinnery Green Mountain Green (120 yards / 2 ounces): 2 (3, 3) hanks Dark (MC); 1 hank Variegated (A)

NEEDLES
One set of five double-pointed needles (dpn) size US 6 (4 mm)

One double-pointed needle, of different color or material, size US 6 (4 mm)

One 24" (60 cm) long circular (circ) needle size US 9 (5.5 mm)

Change needle size if necessary to obtain correct gauge.

NOTIONS
Stitch markers; six 12" pipe cleaners or 20 gauge beading wire 50" (127 cm) long

GAUGE
19 sts and 28 rows = 4" (10 cm) in Stockinette stitch (St st), using smaller needles

STITCH PATTERNS

Textured Pattern (multiple of 10 sts; 1-rnd repeat)
All Rnds: *K7, p3; repeat from * from beginning of Textured Pattern to beginning of Ribbed Band, working pattern through increases and rnd changes (see Notes and instructions).

3x2 Rib (multiple of 5 sts; 1-rnd repeat)
All Rnds: *K3, p2; repeat from * to end.

Biased Rib (odd number of sts; 4-row repeat)
Row 1 (RS): K2tog, *p1, k1; repeat from * to last 3 sts, p1, k1-f/b, k1.
Row 2: Slip 1, *k1, p1; repeat from * to last 2 sts, p2.
Row 3: K2tog, *k1, p1; repeat from * to last 3 sts, k1, p1-f/b, k1.
Row 4: Slip 1, *p1, k1; repeat from * to last 2 sts, p2.
Repeat Rows 1–4 for Biased Rib.

NOTES

This Hat is worked from the top down, beginning with an I-cord and increase rounds. Once you have increased to 10 stitches, you will begin the Textured Pattern and work with six double-pointed needles (dpns), one of which is of a different color. Every time the different-color dpn becomes the working needle (the empty needle in your right hand), you begin the next section (next needle) with an increase. Each round consists of 6 sections (5 same-color dpns plus 1 different-color dpn), therefore each round will begin one needle to the left of

❶ HAT SHAPING

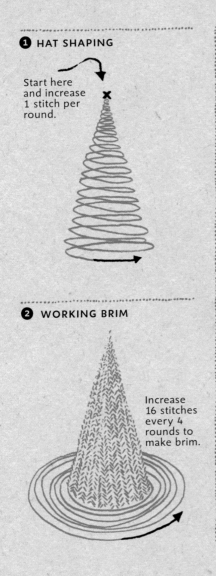

Start here and increase 1 stitch per round.

❷ WORKING BRIM

Increase 16 stitches every 4 rounds to make brim.

where the previous round began. In order for this pattern to work correctly, you must work with 6 dpns.

From the beginning of the Textured Pattern to the beginning of the Ribbed Band, you will work the Textured Pattern without interruption, incorporating increased stitches into the stitch pattern. When working the increases at the beginning of rounds, count the increase as one stitch within the pattern. For example, if you ended the previous round with 5 knit stitches, then the first 2 sts of the next round will complete the k7 that you need for the Textured Pattern. So the M1 should be counted as the sixth stitch of the k7, and the next stitch after the increase will be the seventh; then the following 3 stitches will be purled.

HAT

Using Backward Loop CO (see page 154) and dpn, CO 3 sts, using tail of yarn to CO. Begin I-cord (see page 10); work even for 3 rnds. Divide sts evenly among 3 same-color needles. Join for working in the rnd; do not pm for beginning of rnd.

Note: Each rnd will end 2 sts to the left of where it began.

Rnd 1: M1, k5—4 sts.

Rnd 2: M1, k6—5 sts.

Rnd 3: M1, k7—6 sts.

Rnd 4: M1, k8—7 sts.

Rnd 5: M1, k9—8 sts.

Rnd 6: M1, k10—9 sts.

Rnd 7: M1, k11—10 sts. Divide sts evenly among 5 same-color needles (2 sts each needle).

Begin Textured Pattern

From this point to the Ribbed Band, you will begin every rnd with an increase, and begin every rnd by using the different-color needle as your working needle (the empty needle in your right hand). Every rnd will consist of 6 sections (needles); you will work across the 5 same-color needles, then across the different-color needle, so that you end with the different-color needle empty and in your right hand again; you will end 1 section to the left of where you began the rnd.

Begin Textured Pattern as follows, working st pattern without interruption through increases and rnd changes. Each increase will be considered the next st in the st pattern (see Notes).

Rnd 1: M1, k6, p3, k4—11 sts.

Rnd 2: M1, k2, p3, k7, p2—12 sts.

Rnd 3: M1, k7, p3, k5—13 sts.

Rnd 4: M1, k1, p3, k7, p3, k2—14 sts.

Rnd 5: M1, k4, p3, k7, p3—15 sts.

Rnd 6: M1, k6, p3, k7, p3—16 sts.

Rnd 7: M1, k6, p3, k7, p3, k1—17 sts.

Rnd 8: M1, k5, p3, k7, p3, k3—18 sts.

Rnd 9: M1, k3, p3, k7, p3, k6—19 sts.

Rnd 10: M1, p3, [k7, p3] twice—20 sts.

Rnd 11: M1, k6, p3, k7, p3, k6—21 sts.

Rnd 12: M1, p3, [k7, p3] twice, k3—22 sts.

Rnd 13: M1, k3, p3, [k7, p3] twice, k1—23 sts.

Rnd 14: M1, k5, p3, [k7, p3] twice—24 sts.

Rnd 15: M1, k6, p3, [k7, p3] twice—25 sts (5 sts each needle).

Continue working Textured Pattern and increasing 1 st at the beginning of the rnd every time the different-color needle is the working needle, until you have 16 (18, 20) sts on each needle—80 (90, 100) sts. Place marker for beginning of rnd.

Next Rnd: Change to 3x2 Rib; work even for 8 rnds.

BRIM

SIZE CHILD ONLY

Setup Rnd: Change to circ needle(s). *K1-f/b, k4, pm; repeat from * to end—96 sts (6 sts each section).

SIZE ADULT SMALL ONLY

Setup Rnd: Change to circ needle(s). [K6, pm] 10 times, [k1-f/b, k4, pm] 6 times—96 sts (6 sts each section).

SIZE ADULT LARGE ONLY

Setup Rnd: Change to circ needle(s). [K7, pm] 4 times, [k1-f/b, k5, pm] 12 times—112 sts (7 sts each section).

ALL SIZES

Purl 1 rnd.

Rnd 1: *Knit to 1 st before marker, k1-f/b; repeat from * to end—112 (112, 128) sts [7 (7, 8) sts each section].

Rnds 2, 4, and 6: Purl.

Rnds 3 and 7: Knit.

Rnd 5: *K1-f/b, knit to marker; repeat from * to end—128 (128, 144) sts [8 (8, 9) sts each section].

Rnd 8: Purl.

Repeat Rnds 1–8 until you have 20 (20, 21) sts in each section—320 (320, 336) sts. Purl 1 rnd.

I-Cord BO Rnd: If using pipe cleaners, make a chain approx 50" long by twisting 1" of ends together tightly. Using Knitted CO (see page 155), CO 3 sts to end of left-hand needle; do not turn. *K2, k2tog (1 st from I-cord together with 1 st from Brim), do not turn, slide sts to right-hand end of needle; holding pipe cleaners or beading wire behind needle, bring yarn around behind needle and pipe cleaners/beading wire; repeat from *, pulling yarn from left to right for first st, until all Brim sts have been worked. BO all sts. Join ends of pipe cleaners or beading wire and sew CO and BO edges of I-cord together.

FINISHING

Biased Rib Hatband

CO 15 sts. Purl 1 row. Begin Biased Rib; work even until piece measures 22 (24, 26)" from the beginning, ending with a WS row. BO all sts in pattern. Overlap edges of Hatband to snugly fit wearer's head; sew Hatband to base of Hat, at Ribbed Band.

Solid 1x1 Rib Cap: Blue Sky Alpacas Bulky (50% alpaca / 50% wool; 45 yards / 100 grams): 1 hank #1212 Grasshopper

Variegated 2x2 Rib Cap: Crystal Palace Yarns Mini Mochi (80% merino wool / 20% nylon; 195 yards / 50 grams): 2 hanks #124 Leaves & Sprouts. *Note: This Cap is worked using 2 strands of yarn held together.*

NEEDLES
Solid 1x1 Rib Cap:
One set of four or five double-pointed needles (dpn) size US 15 (10 mm), or one or two 36" (90 cm) long or longer circular (circ) needle(s) size US 15 (10 mm)

Variegated 2x2 Rib Cap:
One set of four or five double-pointed needles (dpn) size US 6 (4 mm), or one or two 36" (90 cm) long or longer circular (circ) needle(s) size US 6 (4 mm)

Change needle size as appropriate for chosen yarn.

NOTIONS
Stitch markers (1 in color A for beginning of rnd; 6 in color B)

swatchless watch cap

Sometimes when I've returned from the yarn shop with a delectable new yarn, the temptation to dive right in and start knitting without first pausing to swatch is just too great. While starting a garment this way could lead to the dreaded "elephant sweater," knitting a snug hat from the center out allows you to dispense with gauge swatching altogether. This simple Watch Cap pattern can be customized to fit any head. The 1x1 Rib Cap (see right) will work in any yarn from sock weight to super-bulky. The 2x2 Rib Cap (see page 43) works best with worsted weight and finer yarns.

STITCH PATTERNS

1x1 Rib (multiple of 2 sts; 1-rnd repeat)
All Rnds: *K1, p1; repeat from * to end.

2x2 Rib (multiple of 4 sts; 1-rnd repeat)
All Rnds: *K2, p2; repeat from * to end.

1x1 RIB CAP
Note: This Cap is suitable for any yarn from sock weight to super bulky.

Using Easy Circular CO or Disappearing Loop CO (see page 148), CO 7 sts. Divide sts among 2 or more needles if necessary for your preferred method of working in the rnd. Join for working in the rnd, being careful not to twist sts; pm (color A) for beginning of rnd.

Shape Crown
Note: Change to circ needle(s) if necessary for number of sts on needle(s).

Rnd 1: *K1-f/b; repeat from * to end—14 sts.

Rnd 2: Purl.

Rnd 3: *K1-f/b, p1; repeat from * to end—21 sts.

Rnd 4: *K2, p1; repeat from * to end.

Rnd 5: *K1-f/b, k1, p1; repeat from * to end—28 sts.

Rnd 6: *K1, p1; repeat from * to end. Place 6 additional markers (color B) every 4 sts.

Rnd 7: *K1-f/b, p1, work in Rib as established to marker; repeat from * to end—35 sts.

Rnd 8: *K2, p1, work in Rib to marker; repeat from * to end.

Rnd 9: *K1-f/b, work in Rib to marker; repeat from * to end—42 sts.

Rnd 10: *K1, p1; repeat from * to end.

Repeat Rnds 7–10, increasing 7 sts each rnd, until piece measures desired width (measured flat at its widest point), comfortably stretched as it will be when worn, ending with Rnd 10.

Work even until piece is desired length. BO all sts in pattern.

FINISHING
Block as desired.

2x2 RIB CAP
Note: This Cap works best with yarns of worsted weight or finer.

Using needle size appropriate for chosen yarn and Easy Circular CO (see page 144) or Disappearing Loop CO (see page 148), CO 7 sts. Divide sts among 2 or more needles if necessary for your preferred method of working in the rnd. Join for working in the rnd, being careful not to twist sts; pm (color A) for beginning of rnd.

Shape Crown
Note: Change to circ needle(s) if necessary for number of sts on needle(s).

Rnd 1: *K1-f/b; repeat from * to end—14 sts.

Rnd 2: Knit.

Rnd 3: *K1, k1-f/b; repeat from * to end—21 sts.

Rnd 4: *K2, p1; repeat from * to end.

Rnd 5: *K1, k1-f/b, p1; repeat from * to end—28 sts.

Rnd 6: *K2, p2; repeat from * to end.

Rnd 7: *K1, k1-f/b, p2; repeat from * to end—35 sts.

Rnd 8: *K3, p2; repeat from * to end.

Rnd 9: *K1, k1-f/b, k1, p2; repeat from * to end—42 sts.

Rnd 10: *K4, p2; repeat from * to end. Place 6 additional markers (color B) every 6 sts.

Rnd 11: [K1, k1-f/b, *k2, p2; repeat from * to marker] 7 times—49 sts.

Rnd 12: *K2, p1, work in Rib as established to marker; repeat from * to end.

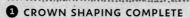

STANDARD HAT SIZES

SIZE	HEAD CIRCUMFERENCE	FLAT WIDTH	LENGTH
Preemie	12"	6"	3 ¾"
Baby	14"	7"	4 ½"
Toddler	16"	8"	5"
Child	18"	9"	5 ¾"
Small adult	20"	10"	6 ¼"
Large adult	22"	11"	7"

❶ CROWN SHAPING COMPLETE

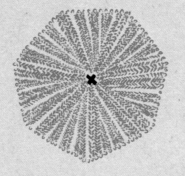

Start at X and increase 7 times every other round until it's big enough.

❷ WORKING TO DESIRED LENGTH

Continue in rib without shaping to desired length.

Rnd 13: *K1, k1-f/b, p1, work in Rib to marker; repeat from * to end—56 sts.

Rnd 14: *K2, p2; repeat from * to end.

Rnd 15: *K1, k1-f/b, p2, work in Rib to marker; repeat from * to end—63 sts.

Rnd 16: *K3, p2, work in Rib to marker; repeat from * to end.

Rnd 17: *K1, k1-f/b, k1, p2, work in Rib to marker; repeat from * to end—70 sts.

Rnd 18: *K4, p2, work in Rib to marker; repeat from * to end.

Repeat Rnds 11–18, increasing 7 sts each rnd, until piece measures desired width (measured flat at its widest point), comfortably stretched as it will be when worn, ending with Rnd 14.

Work even until piece is desired length. BO all sts in pattern.

FINISHING
Block as desired.

VARIATIONS

You may wish to vary the length of the Cap to suit the wearer's preference. If worked on long circular needles, you may try the Cap on as it is worked to check desired fit. The basic shape of this Cap will also work with other combinations of knit and purl—you might wish to personalize your Cap with a different rib pattern, or change the look with a simple knit/purl combination like Seed or Moss stitch.

medallion caps

Mary Thomas's classic *Book of Knitting Patterns* contains a fascinating photograph of more than twenty early eighteenth-century baby bonnets, each of which features a different medallion motif at the crown. There are octagons, squares, stars, flowers, and ruffles to cover the baby's head. I wonder who these long-gone knitters and bonnet-inventors were, and how the infants they covered lived. After studying Thomas's photo I felt inspired to create my own version of the bonnet: Here, a seven-part pinwheel shape dissolves into textured lace to form a star motif. I love the textures and colors this naturally dyed wool yarn adds to each cap. The orange is dyed with madder and the yellow with daffodils.

CROWN

Using Backward Loop CO (see page 154) and tail of yarn, CO 4 sts. Begin I-cord (see page 000); work even for 3 rnds.

Next Rnd: [K1-f/b] 3 times, k1—7 sts. Divide sts among 2 or more needles if necessary for your preferred method of working in the rnd; pm for beginning of rnd.

Rnds 1, 3, 5, 7, and 9: Knit.

Rnd 2: *Yo, k1; repeat from * to end—14 sts.

Rnd 4: *Yo, k2; repeat from * to end—21 sts.

Rnd 6: *Yo, k3; repeat from * to end—28 sts.

Rnd 8: *Yo, k4; repeat from * to end—35 sts.

Rnd 10: *Yo, k5; repeat from * to end—42 sts.

Rnd 11: *Yo, ssk, k4; repeat from * to end.

Rnd 12: *Yo, k6; repeat from * to end—49 sts.

Rnd 13: *Yo, k2tog, yo, ssk, k3; repeat from * to end.

Rnd 14: *Yo, k7; repeat from * to end—56 sts.

Rnd 15: *[Yo, k2tog] twice, yo, ssk, k2; repeat from * to end.

FINISHED MEASUREMENTS
15" circumference

YARN
Solitude Wool Border Leicester (100% wool; 240 yards / 4 ½–5 ounces): 1 hank Undyed, Madder, or Daffodil. *Note: One hank will make several hats.*

NEEDLES
One set of four or five double-pointed needles (dpn), or one or two 36" (90 cm) long or longer circular (circ) needle(s) size US 3 (3.25 mm)

Change needle size if necessary to obtain correct gauge.

NOTIONS
Stitch marker

GAUGE
20 sts and 28 rows = 4" (10 cm) in Stockinette stitch (St st)

CROWN COMPLETED

10 stitches

Rnd 16: *Yo, k8; repeat from * to end—63 sts.

Rnd 17: *[Yo, k2tog] three times, yo, ssk, k1; repeat from * to end.

Rnd 18: *Yo, k9; repeat from * to end—70 sts.

Rnd 19: *[Yo, k2tog] 4 times, yo, ssk; repeat from * to end.

Rnds 20, 22, 24, 26, 28, 30, and 32: Remove beginning-of-rnd marker; slip 1 st, replace beginning-of-rnd marker, *yo, k2tog; repeat from * to end.

Rnds 21, 23, 25, 27, 29, 31, and 33: Knit.

BAND

Rnds 1–8: Knit.

Rnd 9 (Turning Rnd): *Yo, k2tog; repeat from * to end.

Rnd 10: Knit.

Rnd 11: *K8, k2tog; repeat from * to end—63 sts remain.

Rnds 12 and 13: Knit.

FINISHING

Fold hem to WS at Turning Rnd and sew live sts to WS, being careful not to let sts show on RS.

THE NUMBER SEVEN

Early mathematicians loved to construct regular polygons using nothing more than a straight edge and a compass. But you can't do that with the number seven, which is part of what makes seven so special. The ancients called seven the "virgin number," and whether it's used to count noble virtues, deadly sins, notes on the scale, or days of the week, seven is often recognized as a powerful, lucky, or magical number. I've used the number seven in several of the projects in this book: The Medallion Caps featured here and the Watch Caps (page 40) are both divided into seven sections, and you'll also find sevens worked into the construction of the Cone Hats (page 33) and Ripple Baby Blanket (page 123).

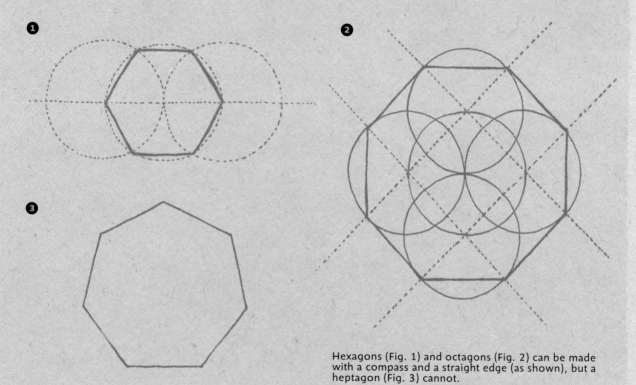

Hexagons (Fig. 1) and octagons (Fig. 2) can be made with a compass and a straight edge (as shown), but a heptagon (Fig. 3) cannot.

half-moon mittens

I call these my "show-off" mittens, since they flummox knitters who try to figure out where construction begins and ends. Here's the secret: You start at the thumb tip and work downward in a tube. At the thumb base, you work increases at eight even points so the fabric forms an octagonal shape. You continue this octagon until it's almost large enough to cover the hand, then work a few short rows to enclose the little fingers. Finally, you work a column of decreases from the fingertip to the cuff, zipping the sides together. Although this column looks like a decorative seam, the mittens are made in one piece without ever breaking the yarn.

STITCH PATTERN

2x2 Rib (multiple of 4 sts; 1-rnd repeat)
All Rnds: *K2, p2; repeat from * to end.

RIGHT MITTEN

Thumb

Using Easy Circular CO (see page 144) or Disappeaing Loop CO (see page 148), CO 5 sts. Divide sts among 2 or more needles if necessary for your preferred method of working in the rnd. Join for working in the rnd, being careful not to twist sts; pm for beginning of rnd.

Rnds 1 and 3: Knit.

Rnd 2: *RLI, k1; repeat from * to end—10 sts.

Rnd 4: *RLI, k2; repeat from * to end—15 sts.

Work even until piece measures 2" from beginning, or to thumb base (see Fig. 1).

Hand

Rnd 1: Knit to last 4 sts, [k1, LLI] 4 times—19 sts.

Rnds 2 and 4: Knit.

Rnd 3: Knit to last 8 sts, [k1, LLI, k1] 4 times—23 sts.

Rnd 5: Knit to last 12 sts, [pm, k1, LLI, pm, k2] 4 times—27 sts [11 sts in first section, 2 sts in remaining sections].

Rnd 6: Knit.

SIZES
Small (Large)

FINISHED MEASUREMENTS
7 (8)" knuckle circumference

YARN
Morehouse Merino 2-ply (100% wool; 220 yards / 2 ounces):
1 hank Henna or Chocolate

NEEDLES
One set of four or five double-pointed needles (dpn) size US 4 (3.5 mm), or one or two 36" (90 cm) long or longer circular (circ) needle(s)

Change needle size if necessary to obtain correct gauge.

NOTIONS
Stitch markers; stitch holders

GAUGE
24 sts and 32 rows = 4" (10 cm) in Stockinette stitch (St st)

Shape Base of Thumb

Rnd 1: Knit to first marker, *k1, LLI, knit to marker; repeat from * to end—35 sts.

Rnd 2: Knit.

Repeat Rnds 1 and 2 until you have 83 (99) sts [11 sts in first section, 9 (11) sts in remaining sections].

Next Round (Partial Rnd): Remove beginning-of-rnd marker. Knit to first marker, transfer last 11 sts worked to st holder, removing marker, don't turn—72 (88) sts remain (see Fig. 2).

Shape Hand

Note: Mitten will be worked back and forth to the tip of the fingers, using short rows. The sections will now be numbered 1–8, from right to left, with RS facing.

Row 1 (RS): [K1, LLI, knit to marker] 7 times, k1, LLI, knit to last 2 sts, wrp-t—8 sts increased; 2 sts out of work.

Row 2: Purl to last 2 sts, wrp-t—2 sts out of work.

Repeat Rows 1 and 2 until you have 16 (20) sts each in Sections 2–7, and 2 active sts remain in sections 1 and 8—100 (124) sts; 14 (18) sts out of work at either end.

With RS facing, transfer first and last 16 (20) sts to separate holders for Cuff [the 14 (18) out-of-work sts from either end, and the 2 remaining active sts each from sections 1 and 8], removing markers—96 (120) sts remain; 43 (51) total sts on all holders (see Fig. 3).

Remove second and fourth markers—3 markers remain, dividing work into 2 sections of 16 (20) sts at each end, and 2 center sections of 32 (40) sts.

Shape Outside Edge

Row 1 (RS): Knit to first marker, remove marker, k8, pm, knit to 4 sts before final marker, turn, leaving last 20 (24) sts on the needle but out of work.

Row 2: Slip 4 sts to right-hand needle, p4, pm, purl to final marker, turn, leaving last 24 (28) sts on the needle but out of work. Remove marker.

Row 3: Slip 4 sts to RH needle [28 (32) sts on right-hand needle but out of work], knit to second marker (placed in Row 2); turn, removing marker, leaving 28 (32) sts on the needle but out of work.

Row 4: Slip 4 sts to right-hand needle [32 (36) sts on right-hand needle but out of work], purl to 1 st after first marker (top center of Mitten), removing marker; turn (see Fig. 4). *Note: Be sure not to pull float tight across back of slipped sts.*

Outside Edge Seam

Next Row (RS): K2tog, *slip 2 sts from right-hand needle back to left-hand needle, s2kp2; repeat from *, removing markers as you come to them, until 1 st remains.

Cuff

Transfer all sts from st holders back to needles—44 (52) sts. Join for working in the rnd; pm for beginning of rnd. Knit 1 rnd, working wraps together with wrapped sts as you come to them.

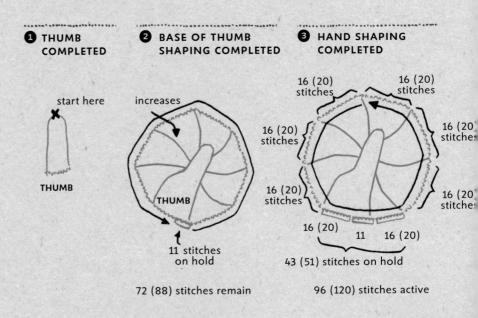

❶ THUMB COMPLETED

start here

✗

THUMB

❷ BASE OF THUMB SHAPING COMPLETED

increases

THUMB

11 stitches on hold

72 (88) stitches remain

❸ HAND SHAPING COMPLETED

16 (20) stitches

16 (20) stitches

16 (20) stitches

16 (20) stitches

16 (20) stitches

16 (20) stitches

16 (20)   11   16 (20)

43 (51) stitches on hold

96 (120) stitches active

Next Rnd: Change to 2x2 Rib; work even until Cuff measures 2". BO all sts in pattern (see Fig. 5).

LEFT MITTEN
Work as for Right Mitten to beginning of Hand.

Hand
Rnd 1: Knit to last 4 sts, [RLI, k1] 4 times—19 sts.

Rnds 2 and 4: Knit.

Rnd 3: Knit to last 8 sts, [k1, RLI, k1] 4 times—23 sts.

Rnd 5: Knit to last 12 sts, [pm, k2, pm, RLI, k1] 4 times—27 sts [11 sts in first section, 2 sts in remaining sections].

Rnd 6: Knit.

Shape Base of Thumb
Rnd 1: Knit to first marker, *knit to 1 st before marker, RLI, k1; repeat from * to end—35 sts.

Rnd 2: Knit.

Repeat Rnds 1 and 2 until you have 83 (99) sts [11 sts in first section, 9 (11) sts in remaining sections].

Next Round (Partial Rnd): Remove beginning of rnd marker. Knit to first marker, transfer last 11 sts worked to st holder, removing marker, don't turn—72 (88) sts remain.

Shape Hand
Note: Mitten will be worked back and forth to the tip of the fingers. The sections will now be numbered 1–8, from right to left, with RS facing.

Row 1: [Knit to 1 st before marker, RLI, k1] 7 times, knit to last 3 sts, RLI, k1, wrp-t—8 sts increased; 2 sts out of work.

Row 2: Purl to last 2 sts, wrp-t—2 sts out of work.

Repeat Rows 1 and 2 until you have 16 (20) sts each in Sections 2–7, and 2 active sts remain in sections 1 and 8—100 (124) sts; 14 (18) sts out of work at either end.

Complete as for Right Mitten.

VARIATIONS

You may modify this pattern to fine tune the fit. At the end of the Shape Base of Thumb section, the Mitten should just reach the wearer's wrist. Repeat Rounds 1 and 2 of that section more or fewer times as needed for the Mitten to reach that point. If you modify this section, ignore the stitch counts of the Shape Hand section, simply repeating Rows 1 and 2 of that section until 2 active stitches remain at either end in sections 1 and 8.

You may also fine tune the fit in the Shape Outside Edge section by working more or fewer short rows— the small fingers should be covered by the fabric before working the outside edge seam.

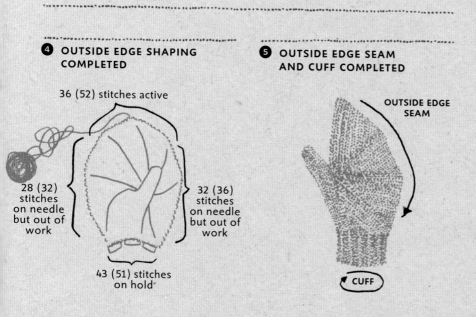

4 **OUTSIDE EDGE SHAPING COMPLETED**

36 (52) stitches active

28 (32) stitches on needle but out of work

32 (36) stitches on needle but out of work

43 (51) stitches on hold

5 **OUTSIDE EDGE SEAM AND CUFF COMPLETED**

OUTSIDE EDGE SEAM

CUFF

radmila's slippers

Throughout Eastern Europe, the held-over Ottoman custom of removing your shoes at home has produced a great variety of knitted slippers. My inspiration for these came from a pair from Bosnia, knitted by the mother of a friend. Radmila's slippers were incredibly colorful to suit her style, and had an intriguing shape. Worked downward from the cuff, they ended with a seam that ran under the foot. I'm a big fan of turning my knitting upside down, so I started my own pair of slippers from the bottom of the foot and worked upward.

NOTES

The Slipper begins as a double-sided line of stitches at the bottom of the Sole. Stitches are increased at regular points, expanding outwards to form the Sole, then decreased to form the Upper, enclosing the toes and foot. As the Slipper takes shape, remember that the side facing you is the Sole.

Instructions are given for women's shoe size 8 and men's shoe size 9. If you are working a size other than the given sizes, consult the sizing table on page 56 for your cast-on number. If you are able to measure the wearer's foot, consult the sidebar on page 55 to determine the cast-on numbers.

LEFT SLIPPER

Sole
Using Figure Eight CO (see page 146) and A, CO 22 (25) sts (or number of sts for your size) onto each needle—44 (50) sts. Place marker (color B) for beginning of rnd; p22 (25) (or the number of sts you CO onto each needle); with second circ needle, purl to end of rnd.

Shape Sole
Rnd 1: *[K1, p1, k1] in 1 st, knit to last st on needle, [k1, p1, k1] in 1 st; repeat from * to end—52 (58) sts.

Rnd 2: *Needle 1:* P1, pm (end Section 1), p2, pm (end Section 2), purl to last 3 sts on needle, pm (end Section 3), p1, pm (end Section 4), p2 (end Section 5); *Needle 2:* P3, pm (end Section 6), purl to last 3 sts on needle, pm (end Section 7), p2, pm (end Section 8), p1 (end Section 9).

SIZES
Women's 8 (Men's 9) (see Notes for instructions on working other sizes)

FINISHED MEASUREMENTS
3" wide at Sole x 7 ½ (8)" long, unstretched. *Note: Slippers will stretch to fit 4" wide x 9 ½ (10 ½)" long.*

YARN
Blue Sky Alpacas Worsted Hand Dyes (50% royal alpaca / 50% merino; 100 yards / 100 grams): 2 hanks #2001 Dungaree Blue (MC) or #2015 Putty (MC); 1 hank #2016 Chocolate (A). *Note: If you will be working a size smaller than women's shoe size 8, you may only need 1 hank of MC.*

NEEDLES
Two 24" (60cm) long circular (circ) needles size US 6 (4 mm)

Change needle size if necessary to obtain correct gauge.

NOTIONS
Stitch markers [including 1 in different color (color B), and 1 removable marker]

GAUGE
20 sts and 26 rows = 4" (10 cm) in Stockinette stitch (St st), unstretched. *Note: Slipper is worked at tighter gauge than yarn calls for, for a thick and cushiony sole.*

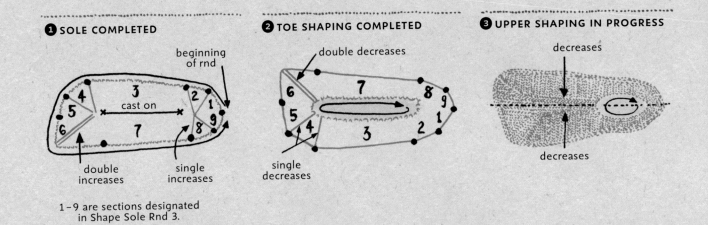

beginning
of rnd

cast on

double
increases

single
increases

1–9 are sections designated
in Shape Sole Rnd 3.

double decreases

single
decreases

decreases

decreases

Rnd 3: *Sections 1 and 2:* Knit to last st in Section, k1-f/b; *Section 3:* Knit; *Sections 4 and 5:* Knit to last st in Section, k1-f/b; *Section 6:* Knit to center st in Section, [k1, p1, k1] in center st, knit to end of Section; *Section 7:* Knit; *Sections 8 and 9:* K1-f/b, knit to end of Section—60 (66) sts (see Fig. 1).

Rnd 4: Purl.

Repeat Rnds 3 and 4, increasing 8 sts each repeat, until you have 108 (114) sts, or until Sole is desired width when comfortably stretched, ending with Rnd 4. Knit 1 rnd. Purl 1 rnd. Break yarn.

Upper

Shape Toe

Rnd 1: Change to MC. *Sections 1–3:* Knit; *Sections 4 and 5:* Ssk, knit to end of Section; *Section 6:* Knit to 1 st before center st, s2kp2, knit to end of Section; *Sections 7–9:* Knit—104 (110) sts remain.

Rnd 2: Knit.

Repeat Rnds 1 and 2, decreasing 4 sts each repeat, until 1 st remains in Section 4, ending with Rnd 2—80 (86) sts remain (see Fig. 2).

Shape Upper

Count number of sts in Section 1; pm that many sts after marker at end of Section 2. Remove all markers except new marker and beginning of rnd marker.

Rnd 1: *Needle 1:* Knit to last 3 sts on needle, k2tog, k1; *Needle 2:* K1, ssk, knit to end—78 (84) sts remain (2 sts decreased) (see Fig. 3).

Repeat Rnd 1 until column of raised sts (k2tog) reaches new marker—54 sts remain.

Knit 4 rnds. BO all sts knitwise.

RIGHT SLIPPER

Work as for Left Slipper to beginning of Sole Shaping.

Shape Sole

Rnd 1: *[K1, p1, k1] in 1 st, knit to last st on needle, [k1, p1, k1] in 1 st; repeat from * to end—52 (58) sts.

Rnd 2: *Needle 1:* P1, pm (end Section 1), p2, pm (end Section 2), purl to last 3 sts on needle, pm (end Section 3), p3 (end Section 4); *Needle 2:* P2, pm (end Section 5), p1, pm (end Section 6), purl to last 3 sts on needle, pm (end Section 7), p2, pm (end Section 8), p1 (end Section 9).

Rnd 3: *Sections 1 and 2:* Knit to last st in Section, k1-f/b; *Section 3:* Knit; *Section 4:* Knit to center st in Section, [k1, p1, k1] in center st, knit to end of Section; *Sections 5 and 6:* Knit to last st in section, k1-f/b; *Section 7:* Knit; *Sections 8 and 9:* K1-f/b, knit to end of Section—60 (66) sts.

Rnd 4: Purl.

Repeat Rnds 3 and 4, increasing 8 sts each repeat, until you have 108 (114) sts, or until Sole is desired width when comfortably stretched, ending with Rnd 4. Knit 1 rnd. Purl 1 rnd. Break yarn.

Upper
Shape Toe

Rnd 1: Change to MC. *Sections 1–3:* Knit; *Section 4:* Knit to 1 st before center st, s2kp2, knit to end of Section; *Sections 5 and 6:* Knit to last 2 sts in Section, k2tog; *Sections 7–9:* Knit—104 (110) sts.

Rnd 2: Knit.

Repeat Rnds 1 and 2 until 1 st remains in Section 4, ending with Rnd 2—80 (86) sts remain.

Complete as for Left Slipper.

CUSTOMIZING CAST-ON NUMBER

If you can, measure the length and width of one foot of the person for whom you are knitting these slippers, at the longest and widest points. Subtract the foot width from the foot length, and multiply the resulting number by 4. Round to a whole number (we rounded down), and cast that number of stitches onto each of the two needles. To adapt these slippers for yarn of a different gauge, subtract the foot width from the foot length, multiply the resulting number by 0.8, then multiply by the Stockinette stitch gauge for one inch. *Note: If you have a wide foot, you might consider casting on fewer stitches so that it takes you longer to get to the necessary slipper length; the more increase rounds you have to work to get to your desired foot length, the wider the sole will be.*

STANDARD SOCK SIZES

CHILD'S SHOE SIZE (ages 1–7)

SHOE SIZE	FOOT LENGTH	FOOT WIDTH	CAST-ON LENGTH	CAST-ON NUMBER
6	5 1/4"	3"	1 3/4"	8
7	5 1/2"	3"	2"	10
8	5 3/4"	3 1/4"	2"	10
9	6 1/4"	3 1/2"	2 1/4"	11
10	6 1/2"	3 3/4"	2 1/4"	11
11	6 3/4"	3 3/4"	2 1/2"	12
12	7 1/4"	4"	2 1/2"	12
13	7 1/2"	4"	2 3/4"	13

WOMEN'S SHOE SIZE (size 8 given in pattern)

SHOE SIZE	FOOT LENGTH	FOOT WIDTH	CAST-ON LENGTH	CAST-ON NUMBER
4	8 1/4"	3 1/2"	3 3/4"	18
5	8 1/2"	3 1/2"	4"	20
6	9"	3 3/4"	4 1/4"	21
7	9 1/4"	3 3/4"	4 1/2"	22
8	9 1/2"	4"	4 1/2"	22
9	10"	4"	4 3/4"	23
10	10 1/4"	4 1/4"	4 3/4"	23

YOUTH SHOE SIZE (ages 7–10)

SHOE SIZE	FOOT LENGTH	FOOT WIDTH	CAST-ON LENGTH	CAST-ON NUMBER
1	7 3/4"	4 1/4"	2 3/4"	13
2	8 1/4"	4 1/4"	3 1/4"	16
3	8 1/2"	4 1/4"	3 1/2"	17
4	8 3/4"	4 1/2"	3 1/2"	17
5	9 1/4"	4 1/2"	3 3/4"	18
6	9 1/2"	4 1/2"	4"	20
7	9 3/4"	4 3/4"	4"	20

MEN'S SHOE SIZE (size 9 given in pattern)

SHOE SIZE	FOOT LENGTH	FOOT WIDTH	CAST-ON LENGTH	CAST-ON NUMBER
6	9 1/4"	3 1/2"	4 1/2"	22
7	9 3/4"	3 1/2"	5"	25
8	10"	3 3/4"	5"	25
9	10 1/4"	4"	5"	25
10	10 1/2"	4"	5 1/4"	26
11	11"	4"	5 1/2"	27
12	11 1/4"	4 1/4"	5 1/2"	27

YARN
Verdant Gryphon Bugga (70%
superwash merino / 20% cashmere /
10% nylon; 412 yards / 4 ounces):
1 hank Bog Fritillary

NEEDLES
One or two 36" (60 cm) long or
longer circular (circ) needle(s) or
one set of four or five double-
pointed needles (dpn) size US 2
(2.75 mm)

Change needle size if necessary to
obtain correct gauge.

GAUGE
28 sts and 36 rows = 4" (10 cm) in
Stockinette stitch (St st)

toe-up socks

Working socks from the center out, starting at the toe, makes it easy to try them on as you go and get a perfect fit. For these socks, you begin with a figure-eight cast-on at the toe, and work upward in the round, increasing until the toe is wide enough to fit your foot, then continue until the sock is long enough to turn the heel.

STITCH PATTERN

Broken Rib (multiple of 2 sts; 2-rnd repeat)
Rnd 1: *K1, p1; repeat from * to end, end k1 if an odd number of sts.
Rnd 2: Knit.
Repeat Rnds 1 and 2 for Broken Rib.

TOE

Using circ needle and Figure Eight CO (see page 146), CO 18 sts. Join for working in the rnd, being careful not to twist sts; pm for beginning of rnd, and after first 9 sts. The first 9 sts will be the instep; the next 9 sts will be the sole.

Rnd 1: [K1, M1-r, knit to 1 st before marker, M1-l, k1] twice—22 sts.

Rnd 2: Knit.

Repeat Rnds 1 and 2 until you have 21 (25) sts between markers—42 (50) sts.

FOOT

Rnd 1: Work in Broken Rib to marker, knit to end.

Rnd 2: Knit.

Work even until piece measures 6¼ (6¾)", or to 2¼ (2¾)" less than desired Foot length from Toe.

GUSSET

Rnd 1: Work in Broken Rib to marker, k1, M1-r, knit to last st, M1-l, k1—44 (52) sts.

Rnd 2: Knit.

Repeat Rnds 1 and 2 until you have 62 (74) sts [21 (25) sts for instep; 41 (49) sts for Gusset].

Shape Gusset

Rnd 1: Work in Broken Rib to marker, k1, M1-r, k9 (11), pm, ssk, k17 (21), k2tog, pm, knit to last st, M1-l, k1.

Rnd 2: Work in Broken Rib to first marker, knit to second marker, ssk, knit to 2 sts before third marker, k2tog, knit to end—60 (72) sts remain [21 (25) sts for instep; 39 (47) sts for Gusset].

Rnd 3: Work in Broken Rib to first marker, k1, M1-r, knit to second marker, ssk, knit to 2 sts before third marker, k2tog, knit to last st, M1-l, k1.

Rnd 4: Rep Row 2—58 (70) sts remain [21 (25) sts for instep; 37 (45) sts for Gusset].

HEEL FLAP

Setup Row (RS): Work in Broken Rib to first marker, k25 (31), removing markers placed on Rnd 1 of Shape Gusset, turn.

Row 1 (WS): Slip 1 wyif, [k1, slip 1 wyif] 5 (7) times, k1, p2tog, turn—57 (69) sts remain [21 (25) sts for instep; 36 (44) sts for Gusset/Heel].

Row 2: Slip 2 wyib, [p1, slip 1 wyib] 5 (7) times, ssk, turn—56 (68) sts remain [21 (25) sts for instep; 35 (43) sts for Gusset/Heel].

Repeat Rows 1 and 2 until you have 21 (25) sts between markers, knit to beginning of rnd marker on final repeat of Row 2—42 (50) sts remain. Working in the rnd, knit 1 rnd.

LEG

Setup Rnd 1: Work in Broken Rib to marker, k4, work in Broken Rib, beginning with p1, to last 4 sts, k4.

Setup Rnd 2: Knit.

Setup Rnd 3: Work in Broken Rib to marker, k2, work in Broken Rib, beginning with p1, to last 2 sts, k2.

Setup Rnd 4: Knit.

Next Rnd: Work in Broken Rib across all sts. Work even until piece measures 6½" from bottom of Heel, ending with Rnd 2 of Broken Rib.

BO Rnd: K1, *yo, k1, pass first 2 sts one at a time over st just worked; repeat from * until all sts have been BO.

FINISHING

Block as desired.

SIZES

To fit women's shoe size 8 (men's shoe size 10)

YARN

Zauberball Crazy (75% wool / 25% nylon; 459 yards / 100 grams): 1 ball #1160 Earth

NEEDLES

One 36" (90 cm) long or longer circular (circ) needle, or one set of four or five double-pointed needles (dpn) size US 1 (2.25 mm)

Change needle size if necessary to obtain correct gauge.

NOTIONS

Stitch marker; waste yarn

GAUGE

32 sts and 44 rows = 4" (10 cm) in Stockinette stitch (St st), using smaller needle and A

heel-up socks

Socks are typically worked from one end to the other—top-down or toe-up. For more adventurous shaping, these start somewhere new—under the ball of the heel (see right).

You begin these by working from the center out, increasing at eight points to make an octagon with eight even sides. Next you extend the left and right sides of the octagon by working back and forth until the sole is as long as your foot. Then you join and work all of the stitches in the round, decreasing at regular points to close the toe. The sides of the foot come together in an origami moment— you stack one centered decrease upon the next, drawing one stitch from either side of the sock like closing a zipper— leaving you with just enough stitches to work the leg.

STITCH PATTERN

3x2 Rib (multiple of 5 sts; 1-rnd repeat)
All Rnds: K1, *p2, k3; repeat from * to last 4 sts, p2, k2.

HEEL

Using smaller needle, and Easy Circular CO (see page 144) or Disappearing Loop CO (see page 148), CO 8 sts. Divide sts among 2 or more needles if necessary for your preferred method of working in the rnd. Join for working in the rnd, being careful not to twist sts; pm for beginning of rnd.

Rnd 1 and all Odd-Numbered Rnds: Knit.

Rnd 2: *RLI, k1; repeat from * to end—16 sts.

Rnd 4: *K2, LLI; repeat from * to end—24 sts.

Rnd 6: *RLI, k3; repeat from * to end—32 sts.

Rnd 8: *K4, LLI; repeat from * to end—40 sts.

Rnd 10: *RLI, k5; repeat from * to end—48 sts.

Rnd 12: *K6, LLI; repeat from * to end—56 sts.

Rnd 14: *RLI, k7; repeat from * to end—64 sts.

Rnd 16: *K8, LLI; repeat from * to end—72 sts.

Rnd 18: *RLI, k9; repeat from * to end—80 sts.

Rnd 20: *K10, LLI; repeat from * to end—88 sts (see Fig. 1).

Rnd 22: Remove beginning of rnd marker, k55 and transfer these sts to waste yarn, RLI, k11, LLI, k11, RLI, k11, LLI, turn—37 sts.

SOLE

Row 1 (WS): Working on 37 Sole sts only, slip first 2 sts to waste yarn, purl to last 2 sts, slip 2 remaining sts to waste yarn—33 sts remain.

Row 2: K1, RLI, k10, LLI, k11, RLI, k10, LLI, k1, turn—37 sts.

Repeat Rows 1 and 2 until piece measures 9½ (10½)", or to desired length from end to end, measured at longest point, ending with a WS row—33 sts [60 (72) sts on waste yarn on each side of Sole] (see Fig. 2).

Next Rnd: Transfer sts from waste yarn for left side of Sole to one spare needle, sts from waste yarn for Heel to second spare needle, and sts from waste yarn for right side of Sole to a third spare needle. *Note: If you are using a circ needle, you may transfer all sts to left-hand end of circ needle in the following order, following sts left after Row 2 above: Sts for left side of Sole, sts for Heel, sts for right side of Sole.* Change to working in the rnd; place marker for new beginning of rnd. K1, RLI, k10, LLI, k11, RLI, k10, LLI, k1, *with right-hand needle, pick up float from behind slipped st and place it on left-hand needle, k2tog (picked-up float and

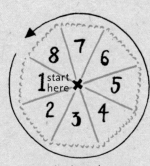

❶ HEEL

88 (60) stitches

❷ SOLE IN PROGRESS

33 active stitches

increases

60 (72) stitches on hold

60 (72) stitches on hold

55 (35) stitches on hold

next st on needle), k1*; repeat from * to * until all slipped sts on this side of Sole are worked, knit across Heel sts, **pick up strand between last st worked and first slipped st as if to M1, k2tog (picked-up strand and next st on needle), k1**; repeat from ** to ** to end of rnd—212 (236) sts.

TOE

Rnds 1 and 2: Knit.

Rnd 3: Ssk, k9, k2tog, k11, ssk, k9, k2tog, knit to end—208 (232) sts remain.

Rnd 4: Ssk, k7, k2tog, k11, ssk, k7, k2tog, knit to end—204 (228) sts remain.

Rnd 5: Ssk, k5, k2tog, k11, ssk, k5, k2tog, knit to end—200 (224) sts remain.

Rnd 6: Ssk, k3, k2tog, k11, ssk, k3, k2tog, knit to end—196 (220) sts remain.

Rnd 7: Ssk, k1, k2tog, k11, ssk, k1, k2tog, knit to end—192 (216) sts remain.

Rnd 8: S2kp2, k11, s2kp2, knit to last 5 sts, place marker for new beginning of rnd—188 (212) sts remain.

Rnd 9: Knit, removing old beginning-of-rnd marker.

Rnd 10: K4, s2kp2, k9, s2kp2, knit to end—184 (208) sts remain.

Rnds 11, 13, 15, and 17: Knit.

Rnd 12: K3, s2kp2, k7, s2kp2, knit to end—180 (204) sts remain.

Rnd 14: K2, s2kp2, k5, s2kp2, knit to end—176 (200) sts remain.

Rnd 16: K1, s2kp2, k3, s2kp2, knit to end—172 (196) sts remain.

Rnd 18: S2kp2, k1, s2kp2, knit to end—168 (192) sts remain.

Rnd 19: Knit, removing beginning-of-rnd marker (see Fig. 3).

UPPER

Zip Sides: *S2kp2 (creating a raised decrease st), slip 2 sts from right-hand needle back to left-hand needle; repeat from * until 104 sts remain (see Fig. 4).

Upper Gusset: *S2kp2, knit to 1 st before raised decrease st—2 sts decreased each rnd; repeat from * until 64 sts remain, place marker for new beginning of rnd (see Fig. 5).

CUFF

Next Rnd: Change to 3x2 Rib, increase 1 st on first rnd—65 sts. Work even until Cuff measures 4" from beginning, or to desired length. BO all sts in pattern.

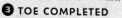

❸ TOE COMPLETED

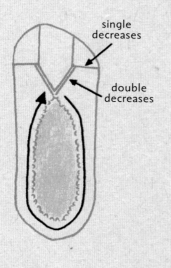

single decreases

double decreases

❹ ZIP SIDES COMPLETED

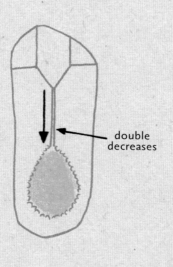

double decreases

❺ UPPER COMPLETED

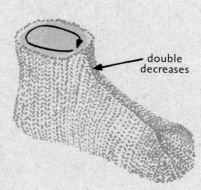

double decreases

swoosh socks

These over-the-knee socks incorporate intentionally dropped stitches into every element of their construction. The toes and heels are shaped by taking into account the added width of dropped-stitch ladders. After working the foot, you knit the legs as skinny tubes of Stockinette stitch. Then, just before the hem, you drop every third stitch off the needles, and unravel the whole way down to the bottom—swoosh! The incredibly stretchy nature of the dropped-stitch fabric allows these socks to expand to fit legs of many dimensions, even though they begin with only thirty-six stitches.

Since intentionally dropping such a long column of stitches is a high stakes venture, I've incorporated occasional purls into the columns that will be dropped to help you keep your place—the purls will disappear as they unravel.

STITCH PATTERN

Dropped Stitch Pattern (for gauge swatch)
Using larger needles, CO 14 sts.
Setup Row (RS): K2, *yo, k2; repeat from * to end.
Begin St st, beginning with a purl row. Work even until piece measures 5" from the beginning, ending with a WS row.
Drop Row (RS): *K2, drop 1 st and unravel down to yo; repeat from * to last 2 sts, k2. Cut yarn, leaving 8" tail. Thread tail through remaining sts, leaving sts loose. Measure gauge at top of swatch.

NOTES

Because there are few hiding places for yarn ends in the very open dropped-stitch fabric, begin the second Sock with a new hank. If you encounter any knots, join them as unobtrusively as possible.

TOE

Using smaller circ needle and Figure Eight CO (see page 146), CO 16 sts. Divide sts among 2 or more needles if necessary for your preferred method of working in the rnd. Join for working in the rnd, being careful not to twist sts. Place marker for beginning of rnd and after 8 sts.

SIZE

To fit women's sock size 8

FINISHED MEASUREMENTS

8" Foot circumference;
22" Thigh circumference;
9 ½" Foot length from back of Heel;
24" Leg length to base of Heel

YARN

ShiBui Knits Staccato (65% superwash merino / 30% silk / 5% nylon; 191 yards / 50 grams): 2 hanks #ST111 Bordeaux

NEEDLES

One set of four or five double-pointed needles (dpn) sizes US 6 (4 mm) and US 1 (2.25 mm), or one or two 36" (90 cm) long or longer circular (circ) needle(s) sizes US 6 (4 mm) and US 1 (2.25 mm)

Change needle size if necessary to obtain correct gauge.

NOTIONS

Stitch markers; 1 yard ⅜" wide elastic; sewing needle and thread

GAUGE

28 sts and 44 rows = 4" (10 cm) in Stockinette stitch (St st), using smaller needles, after washing and blocking

9 sts and 26 rows = 4" (10 cm) in Dropped Stitch Pattern, using larger needles

Rnd 1 and All Odd-Numbered Rnds: Knit.

Rnd 2: K1, M1-r, k6, M1-l, k1; repeat from * to end—20 sts.

Rnd 4: K1, M1-r, k8, M1-l, k2, M1-r, k3, yo, k2, yo, k3, M1-l, k1—26 sts.

Rnd 6: K1, M1-r, k10, M1-l, k2, M1-r, k12, M1-l, k1—30 sts.

Rnd 8: K1, M1-r, k12, M1-l, k2, M1-r, k5, p1, k2, p1, k5, M1-l, k1—34 sts.

Rnd 10: K1, M1-r, k14, M1-l, k19—36 sts.

Rnd 12: K1, M1-r, k16, M1-l, k8, p1, k2, p1, k7—38 sts.

Rnd 14: K1, M1-r, k18, M1-l, k19—40 sts.

Rnd 16: K1, M1-r, k20, M1-l, k8, p1, k2, p1, k7—42 sts.

FOOT

Rnds 1–3: Knit.

Rnd 4: K31, p1, k2, p1, k7.

Repeat Rnds 1–4 until piece measures 7½" from the beginning, or to 2" less than desired Foot length.

GUSSET

Rnd 1: K24, yo, k7, p1, k2,,p1, k7, yo—44 sts.

Rnds 2–7 and 9–14: Knit.

Rnd 8: K27, yo, k5, p1, k2, p1, k5, yo, k3—46 sts.

Rnd 15: K30, yo, k3, p1, k2, p1, k3, yo, k6—48 sts.

Rnds 16–21: Knit. Remove marker after Rnd 21.

HEEL FLAP

Note: Heel Flap is worked back and forth for 6 rows, then rejoined to Gusset by working a full rnd on the seventh row. After each joining rnd, you will increase the width of the Heel Flap by working 2 additional sts on each side of the Heel Flap.

Row 1: (RS) Ssk, k9, yo, k2, yo, k9, k2tog, turn.

Row 2: P2tog, p20, p2tog-tbl, turn.

Row 3: Ssk, k18, k2tog, turn.

Row 4: P2tog, k16, p2tog-tbl, turn.

Row 5: K7, p1, k2, p1, k7, turn.

Row 6: P18, turn.

Rnd 7 (Join): Change to working in the rnd. K7, p1, k2, p1, k7, drop 1 st and unravel down to yo in Row 1, k9, p1, k2, p1, k9, drop 1 st and unravel down to yo in Row 1—40 sts remain.

Row 8: (RS) K20, turn.

Rows 9, 11, and 13: P22, turn.

Rows 10 and 12: K22, turn.

Rnd 14 (Join): Change to working in the rnd. K9, p1, k2, p1, k9, drop 1 st and unravel down to yo in Row 1, k16, drop 1 st and unravel down to yo in Row 1, k2—38 sts remain.

Row 15: K24, turn

Rows 16, 18, and 20: P26, turn.

Rows 17 and 19: K26, turn.

Rnd 21 (Join): K11, p1, k2, p1, k11, drop 1 st and unravel down to yo, k10, drop 1 st and unravel down to yo, k4—36 sts remain. Place marker for new beginning of rnd.

ANKLE

Rnds 1–4 and 6–9: Knit.

Rnd 5: K7, p1, k2, p1, k14, p1, k2, p1, k7.

Rnd 10: *[K1, yo, ssk] twice, k1, p1, k2, p1, k1, [k2tog, yo, k1] twice; repeat from * to end.

Rnd 11: Knit.

LEG

Rnd 1: Change to larger needles. K1, *p1, k2; repeat from * to last 2 sts, p1, k1.

Rnds 2–5: Knit.

Repeat Rnds 1–5 until piece measures 23" from beginning of Heel Flap.

HEM

Rnd 1: Change to smaller needles. K1, *drop 1 st and unravel to yo worked below, CO 5 sts using Backward Loop CO (see page 154), k2; repeat from * to last 2 sts, drop 1 st and unravel to yo worked below, CO 5 sts, k1—84 sts.

Rnds 1–8: Knit.

Rnd 9 (Turning Rnd): *K1, p1; repeat from * to end.

Rnd 10: Knit.

Rnd 11: *K2tog, k8; repeat from * to last 4 sts, k4—74 sts remain.

Rnds 12–15: Knit.

FINISHING

Cut length of elastic ½" wider than desired thigh circumference. Overlap ends ¼" and sew together. Fold Hem over elastic to WS at Turning Rnd and sew in place, being careful not to catch elastic, nor to let sts show on RS.

TOYS

Toys are wonderful projects to try when experimenting or teaching yourself new techniques. Unlike a garment that is destined to be worn, a toy can take any shape you can imagine and create and doesn't have to fit anyone. For me, the radial symmetry built into revolutionary knitting led naturally to creating many-legged creatures like the octopi and starfish in this chapter. The teddy bear here is an adventure in seam-minimizing shaping.

octopus

This playful creature is a wonder of center-out shaping. You begin by making an octagonal underbelly. Then you work the head as a large, flat octagon (like the pinwheel blanket on page 12). You transform the flat fabric into a dome by working pleats into each of the eight sides. Then you attach the head to the underbelly, and work tentacles in the round, gradually tapering them to a point.

   Like most knitted toys, this octopus can be worked with many different yarns, and precise gauge measurements are not essential. Each of the three octopi shown follows the same pattern stitch for stitch, but they are worked with yarns of different weight, from dk to bulky (see page 75).

UNDERBELLY

Using Disappearing Loop CO (see page 148) or Easy Circular CO (see page 144), CO 8 sts. Divide sts among 2 or more needles if necessary for your preferred method of working in the rnd. Join for working in the rnd, being careful not to twist sts; pm (color A) for beginning of rnd.

Note: Change to circ needle(s) if necessary for number of sts on needle(s).

Rnd 1: Knit.

Rnd 2: *K1-f/b; repeat from * to end—16 sts.

Rnd 3: *K1-f/b, k1; repeat from * to end—24 sts.

Rnd 4: *K1-f/b, k2; repeat from * to end—32 sts. Place 7 additional markers (color B) every 4 sts.

Rnd 5: *K1-f/b, knit to marker; repeat from * to end—40 sts.

Repeat Rnd 5 until you have 10 sts between markers—80 sts (see Fig. 1). Transfer sts to waste yarn and set aside.

HEAD

Using Disappearing Loop CO or Easy Circular CO, CO 8 sts. Divide sts among 2 or more needles if necessary for your preferred method of working in the rnd. Join for working in the rnd, being careful not to twist sts; pm (color A) for beginning of rnd.

SIZES
Small (Medium, Large)

FINISHED MEASUREMENTS
16 ½ (18, 26)" Head circumference
Approximately 16 (18, 25)" from Head to tip of Tentacles

YARN
2 (2, 4) hanks (see page 75 for yarns used)

NEEDLES
One set of four or five double-pointed needles (dpns); one 16" (40 cm) long and one or two 36" (90 cm) long circular (circ) needles size US 2 (4, 7) [2.75 (3.5, 4.5) mm]

Change needle size if necessary to obtain correct gauge.

NOTIONS
Stitch markers (1 in color A for beginning of rnd, 7 in color B); polyester or cotton stuffing; ½" safety eyes, buttons, or embroidery floss

GAUGE
26 (24, 15) sts and 32 (30, 20) rows = 4" (10 cm) in Stockinette stitch (St st), using yarn and needles for chosen size. *Note: Gauge is worked tighter than yarn calls for so stuffing is not visible when Octopus is stuffed. If substituting yarn, work with needles a size or two smaller than yarn company recommends to achieve a tight fabric.*

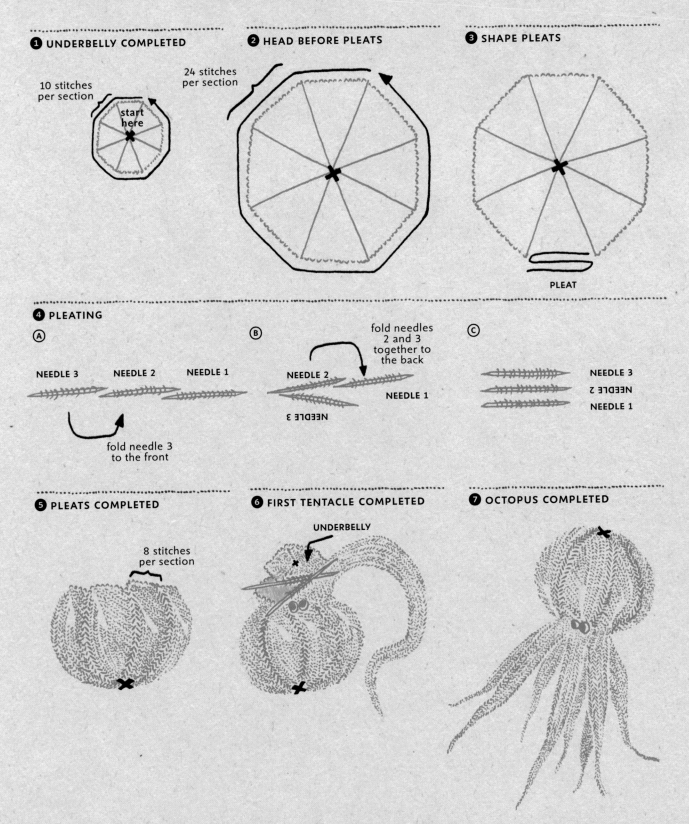

1 UNDERBELLY COMPLETED

10 stitches
per section

24 stitches
per section

start here

2 HEAD BEFORE PLEATS

3 SHAPE PLEATS

PLEAT

4 PLEATING

Ⓐ

NEEDLE 3   NEEDLE 2   NEEDLE 1

fold needle 3
to the front

Ⓑ

NEEDLE 2

fold needles
2 and 3
together to
the back

NEEDLE 1

NEEDLE 3

Ⓒ

NEEDLE 3
NEEDLE 2
NEEDLE 1

5 PLEATS COMPLETED

8 stitches
per section

6 FIRST TENTACLE COMPLETED

UNDERBELLY

7 OCTOPUS COMPLETED

Note: Change to circ needle(s) if necessary for number of sts on needle(s).

Rnds 1, 3, 5, and 7: Knit.

Rnd 2: *K1-f/b; repeat from * to end—16 sts.

Rnd 4: *K1-f/b, k1; repeat from * to end—24 sts.

Rnd 6: *K1-f/b, k2; repeat from * to end—32 sts. Place 7 additional markers (color B) every 4 sts.

Rnd 8: *K1-f/b, knit to marker; repeat from * to end—40 sts.

Rnd 9: Knit.

Repeat Rnds 8 and 9 until you have 24 sts between markers—192 sts (see Fig. 2).

Shape Pleats

Note: Transfer to shorter circ needle, then dpns when necessary for number of sts on needle.

Step 1: Transfer next 24 sts evenly to 3 empty dpns (8 sts each needle), leaving remaining sts on original needle (see Fig. 4A).

Step 2: Fold far left-hand dpn to the front, so that it is parallel to the middle dpn (see Fig. 4B), then fold both needles together to the back, so they are parallel to the first dpn (see Fig. 4C).

Step 3: [K3tog (1 st from each dpn)] 8 times—16 sts decreased.

Repeat Steps 1–3 until you have 8 pleats—64 sts remain. Place marker every 8 sts, placing color A marker at beginning of rnd (see Fig. 5).

Decrease Rnd: *Knit to 2 sts before marker, k2tog; repeat from * to end—56 sts remain.

Repeat Decrease Rnd every rnd until 4 sts remain between markers—32 sts.

Knit 4 rnds. Attach safety eyes or buttons (see photo), or embroider eyes.

Increase Rnd: *RLI, k1; repeat from * to end—64 sts.

TENTACLES

With WSs together (RSs facing out), lay Underbelly on top of Head, with tail from Underbelly across from working yarn attached to Head.

First Tentacle

Transfer 10 sts of Underbelly and first 8 sts of Head to 3 dpns (6 sts each), so that first st of Head is at beginning of rnd, leaving remaining sts on original needles—18 sts. Place marker between fifth and sixth sts of Underbelly to mark bottom center of Tentacle. Join for working in the rnd; pm for beginning of rnd.

Working on these 18 sts only, knit 15 rnds.

Decrease Rnd: Knit to 2 sts before marked center center st, k2tog, slip marker, ssk, knit to end—16 sts remain. Knit 10 rnds.

Repeat Decrease Rnd every 10 rnds until 4 sts remain. Continuing in I-cord (see page 10), work even for 10 rnds. Break yarn, thread through remaining sts, pull tight, and fasten off (see Fig. 6).

Remaining Tentacles

Work as for First Tentacle, stuffing Head and Tentacles after completing seventh Tentacle. Stuff final Tentacle as it is worked.

FINISHING

With tail at beginning of each Tentacle, close gaps between Tentacles.

YARN CHOICES

The three octupi shown on page 72 were made using different weights of yarn to demonstrate the versatility of the pattern: **Small:** Blue Sky Alpacas Melange (100% baby alpaca; 110 yards / 50 grams): 2 hanks #811 Bubblegum; **Medium:** Alisha Goes Around Stable of Horses Worsted (100% superwash merino wool; 200 yards / 100 grams): 2 hanks Wheat; **Large:** O-Wool Legacy Bulky (100% certified organic merino wool; 106 yards / 100 grams): 4 hanks #1000 Natural)

Whatever yarn you work with, choose needles a size or two smaller than the yarn manufacturer's recommendation to achieve a tight fabric so that the stuffing does not show through.

starfish

Like a brain-teasing puzzle that asks you to connect the dots of a drawing without lifting the pencil, the challenge I set for myself in designing this starfish was to create a three-dimensional star shape without ever breaking the yarn. You begin by casting on and increasing at five regular points to create a pentagon. Then, one by one, you work each side of the pentagon back and forth to form the leg. You increase at the center while slipping stitches at either side, creating two sections of stitches held in reserve on either side of each leg. Then you join these reserved stitches with a three-needle bind-off from the tip the whole way back to the center.

SPECIAL TECHNIQUE

Three-Needle BO: Hold dpns parallel to each other with WSs together. Using third dpn with single st, *k2tog (1 st from front needle together with 1 st from back needle), pass first st over second to BO 1 st; repeat from * until 1 st remains.

BODY

Using Easy Circular CO or Disappearing Loop CO (see page 148), CO 10 sts. Join for working in the rnd, being careful not to twist sts; pm (color A) for beginning of rnd. Divide work into 5 sections (2 sts each section), either by placing markers or by dividing sts among 5 dpns, with 1 section per dpn.

Rnd 1 and all Odd-Numbered Rnds: Knit.

Rnd 2: *K1, M1-r, k1; repeat from * to end—15 sts.

Rnd 4: *K1, M1-l, k1, M1-r, k1; repeat from * to end—25 sts.

Rnd 6: *K2, M1-l, k1, M1-r, k2; repeat from * to end—35 sts.

Rnd 8: *K3, M1-l, k1, M1-r, k3; repeat from * to end—45 sts.

Rnd 10: *K4, M1-l, k1, M1-r, k4; repeat from * to end—55 sts.

Rnd 12: *K5, M1-l, k1, M1-r, k5; repeat from * to end—65 sts.

Rnd 14: *K6, M1-l, k1, M1-r, k6; repeat from * to end—75 sts.

Rnd 16: *K7, M1-l, k1, M1-r, k7; repeat from * to end—85 sts.

Rnd 18: *K8, M1-l, k1, M1-r, k8; repeat from * to end—95 sts (19 sts per section).

SIZES
Small (Large)

FINISHED MEASUREMENTS
Approximately 12 (19)" wide

YARN
Spud & Chloe Sweater (55% superwash wool / 45% organic cotton; 160 yards / 100 grams): 1 hank #7501 Popsicle (#7512 Watermelon)

NEEDLES
One set of four, five, or six double-pointed needles (dpn), size US 5 (3.75 mm), or one or two 36" (90 cm) long or longer circular (circ) needle(s) size US 5 (3.75 mm)

Change needle size if necessary to obtain correct gauge.

NOTIONS
Stitch markers

GAUGE
20 sts and 30 rows = 4" (10 cm) in Stockinette stitch (St st).
Note: Gauge is not essential for this project.

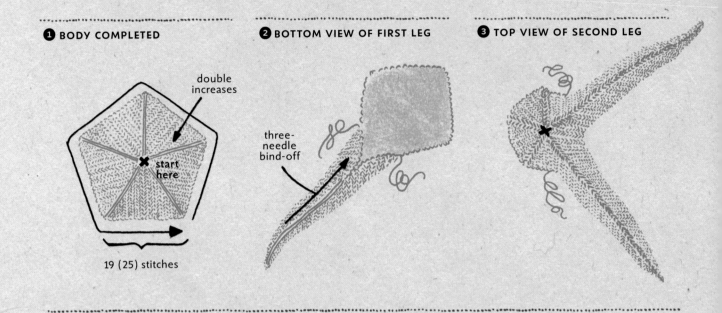

1 BODY COMPLETED

double increases

start here

19 (25) stitches

2 BOTTOM VIEW OF FIRST LEG

three-needle bind-off

3 TOP VIEW OF SECOND LEG

Rnd 19: Knit (see Fig. 1).

SIZE LARGE ONLY

Rnd 20: *K9, M1-l, k1, M1-r, k9; repeat from * to end—105 sts.

Rnd 22: *K10, M1-l, k1, M1-r, k10; repeat from * to end—115 sts.

Rnd 24: *K11, M1-l, k1, M1-r, k11; repeat from * to end—125 sts (25 sts per section).

Rnd 25: Knit (see Fig. 1).

FIRST LEG

BOTH SIZES

Transfer last 76 (100) sts worked to waste yarn. Change to working back and forth.

Setup Row (RS): K2, M1-l, k7 (10), M1-l, k1, M1-r, k7 (10), M1-r, k2—23 (29) sts.

Row 1 and all WS Rows: Slip 1 to st holder or waste yarn, purl to last st, slip 1 to separate st holder or waste yarn; turn—2 sts decreased.

Note: On all following rows, when a st is to be slipped, slip it to the same st holder or waste yarn as the other slipped sts on the same end of the row.

Rows 2, 4, and 6: Slip 1, k2, M1-l, k7 (10), M1-l, k1, M1-r, k7 (10), M1-r, k2, slip 1, turn—23 (29) sts after Row 6.

SIZE LARGE ONLY

Row 8: Slip 1, k2, M1-l, k21, M1-r, k2, slip 1, turn.

Row 10: Slip 1, k2, M1-l, k9, M1-l, k1, M1-r, k9, M1-r, k2, slip 1, turn—27 sts.

Row 12: Slip 1, k2, M1-l, k19, M1-r, k2, slip 1, turn.

Row 14: Slip 1, k2, M1-l, k8, M1-l, k1, M1-r, k8, M1-r, k2, slip 1, turn—25 sts.

Row 16: Slip 1, k2, M1-l, k17, M1-r, k2, slip 1, turn.

BOTH SIZES

Row 7 (17): Repeat Row 1.

Row 8 (18): Slip 1, k2, M1-l, k7, M1-l, k1, M1-r, k7, M1-r, k2, slip 1, turn—23 sts.

Row 10 (20): Slip 1, k2, M1-l, k15, M1-r, k2, slip 1.

Row 12 (22): Slip 1, k2, M1-l, k6, M1-l, k1, M1-r, k6, M1-r, k2, slip 1—21 sts.

Row 14 (24): Slip 1, k2, M1-l, k13, M1-r, k2, slip 1, turn—19 sts.

Row 16 (26): Slip 1, k2, M1-l, k5, M1-l, k1, M1-r, k5, M1-r, k2, slip 1, turn—19 sts.

Row 18 (28): Slip 1, k2, M1-l, k11, M1-r, k2, slip 1, turn.

Row 20 (30): Slip 1, k2, M1-l, k4, M1-l, k1, M1-r, k4, M1-r, k2, slip 1, turn—17 sts.

Row 22 (32): Slip 1, k2, M1-l, k9, M1-r, k2, slip 1, turn.

Row 24 (34): Slip 1, k2, M1-l, k3, M1-l, k1, M1-r, k3, M1-r, k2, slip 1, turn—15 sts.

Row 26 (36): Slip 1, k2, M1-l, k7, M1-r, k2, slip 1, turn.

Row 28 (38): Slip 1, k2, M1-l, k2, M1-l, k1, M1-r, k2, M1-r, k2, slip 1, turn—13 sts.

Row 30 (40): Slip 1, k2, M1-l, k5, M1-r, k2, slip 1, turn.

Row 32 (42): Slip 1, k2, M1-l, k1, M1-l, k1, M1-r, k1, M1-r, k2, slip 1, turn—11 sts.

Row 34 (44): Slip 1, k2, M1-l, k3, M1-r, k2, slip 1, turn.

Row 36 (46): Slip 1, k2, M1-l, k1, M1-r, k2, slip 1, turn.

Row 38 (48): Slip 1, k3, slip 1, turn—3 sts remain.

Row 39 (49): Slip 1, p1, slip 1, turn—1 st remains.

With RS facing, transfer slipped sts to separate dpns; the single remaining st from Row 49 will be on a third dpn (see Fig. 2). Using Three-Needle BO, BO all slipped sts. Fasten off. Do not break yarn. Stuff Leg.

REMAINING LEGS

Transfer next 19 (25) sts from st holder for Body to needle—20 (26) sts.

Setup Row (RS): K2tog (final st from previous leg together with first transferred st), k1, M1-l, k7 (10), M1-l, k1, M1-r, k7 (10), M1-r, k2—23 (29) sts. Complete as for First Leg (see Fig. 3), stuffing final Leg through opening at center of Body.

FINISHING

Sew center Body opening closed.

VARIATIONS

This pattern also looks wonderful when the fabric is worked in stripes, and I could imagine it in other colorwork patterns as well. Like all seamless toys, this Starfish could easily be made larger or smaller by following the pattern as written and using yarn of a different gauge. Remember that variations will also affect yarn requirements. Whatever yarn you choose, use needles one or two sizes smaller than the yarn manufacturer recommends to achieve a tight fabric that won't show the stuffing beneath. If you wish to scale the pattern to a different size, continue the Body pattern until you have created a pentagon of desired size, then complete the legs as follows:

Setup Row (RS): K2, M1-l, knit to 1 st before center st, M1-l, pm, k1, M1-r, knit to last 2 sts, M1-r, k2 — 4 sts increased.

Row 1: Slip 1 to st holder or waste yarn, purl to last st, slip 1 to separate st holder or waste yarn; turn— 2 sts decreased.

Note: On all following rows, when a st is to be slipped, slip it to the same st holder or waste yarn as the other slipped sts on the same end of the row.

Row 2: Slip 1, k2, M1-l, knit to 1 st before center marker, M1-l, sm, k1, M1-r, knit to last 3 sts, M1-r, k2, slip 1, turn— 2 sts increased.

Row 3: Repeat Row 1.

Rows 4–7: Repeat Rows 2 and 3 —no net change in st count after Row 7.

Row 8: Slip 1, k2, M1-l, knit to last 3 sts, M1-r, k2, slip 1, turn—no change in st count.

Row 9: Repeat Row 1.

Repeat Rows 6–9 until 1 st remains. Continue as for Remaining Legs, above, beginning Setup Rows for remaining Legs with k2tog, k1 instead of k2.

You can create longer, skinnier Legs by working more repeats of Rows 6 and 7, which give you a net increase of 0 stitches; or create shorter, fatter Legs by working more repeats of Rows 8 and 9, which give you a net decrease of 2 stitches.

teddy bear

Look closely at the arms, legs, rump, and head of this bear and you'll find pentagons everywhere. Those pentagons are combined in several different ways to shape the bear. You begin by creating a pentagon for the rump, then join the legs to four of the five sides of that pentagon, giving the bear his sturdy, seated posture. You work the body in the round, then form the shoulders and arms by picking up stitches from the back and chest. The head begins as yet another large pentagon that draws together to form the nose and snout. Sound complicated? I've included diagrams to help you through each step of the process.

FINISHED MEASUREMENTS
14" high

YARN
Brooklyn Tweed Shelter (100% Targhee-Columbia wool; 140 yards / 50 grams): 3 hanks #16 Nest

NEEDLES
One set of six double-pointed needles (dpn) size US 6 (4 mm), or one or two 36" (90 cm) long or longer circular (circ) needle(s) size US 6 (4 mm)

Change needle size if necessary to obtain correct gauge.

NOTIONS
Stitch markers; waste yarn; two ¾" sew-on eyes; polyester or cotton stuffing; small amount of contrasting color brown yarn, for nose

GAUGE
18 sts and 28 rows = 4" (10 cm) in Stockinette stitch (St st)

RUMP

Using Easy Circular CO (see page 144) or Disappearing Loop CO (see page 148), CO 5 sts. Join for working in the rnd, being careful not to twist sts; pm for beginning of rnd.

Rnd 1: *K1-f/b; repeat from * to end—10 sts.

Rnd 2: *K1, k1-f/b; repeat from * to end—15 sts. Divide work into 5 sections (3 sts per section), either by placing markers or by dividing sts among 5 dpns, with 1 section per dpn.

Rnd 3: *K1-f/b, knit to end of section; repeat from * to end—20 sts.

Rnd 4: *Knit to last st of section, k1-f/b; repeat from * to end—25 sts.

Rnd 5: Knit.

Rnds 6 and 8: Repeat Rnd 3—40 sts after Rnd 8.

Rnds 7 and 9: Repeat Rnd 4—45 sts after Rnd 9.

Rnd 10: Knit.

Repeat Rnds 6–10 until you have 75 sts (15 sts per section). Break yarn. Transfer 60 sts to waste yarn for Lower Back. Transfer remaining 15 sts to separate waste yarn for Crotch (see Fig. 1).

LEFT LEG

Work as for Rump through Rnd 10—45 sts.

Rnd 11: Repeat Rnd 3—50 sts (10 sts per section).

Rnd 12: *K1, p1; repeat from * to end.

Rnds 13–32: Knit. Transfer first 30 sts (sections 1–3) to waste yarn, turn (see Fig. 2).

LOWER BACK

Join Left Leg to Rump

Transfer 60 sts from waste yarn for Rump to left-hand end of Left Leg needle, leaving last 15 sts on waste yarn—80 sts.

Row 1 (WS): P19, p2tog-tbl (1 st from Left Leg together with 1 st from Rump), turn (see Fig. 3).

Row 2: Slip 1 Rump st to left-hand needle, ssk (slipped st together with 1 Left Leg st), knit to end, turn.

Repeat Rows 1 and 2 until all 60 transferred sts of Rump have been worked; do not turn after final row—20 sts remain.

MAKING THE TEDDY BEAR

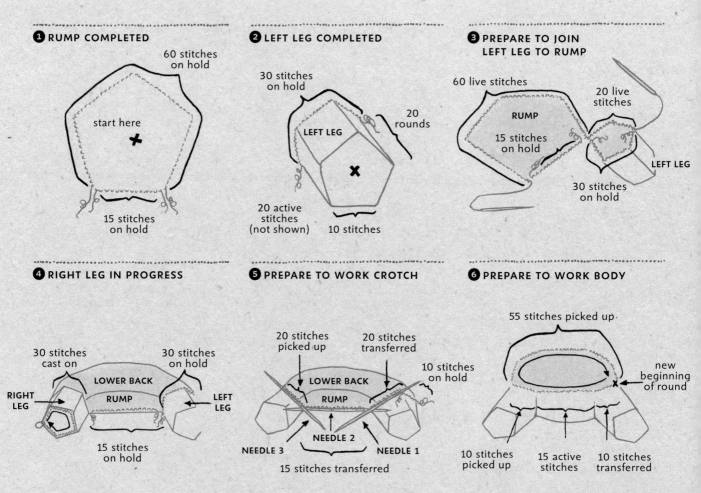

❶ RUMP COMPLETED

60 stitches on hold

start here

15 stitches on hold

❷ LEFT LEG COMPLETED

30 stitches on hold

LEFT LEG

20 rounds

20 active stitches (not shown)

10 stitches

❸ PREPARE TO JOIN LEFT LEG TO RUMP

60 live stitches

20 live stitches

RUMP

15 stitches on hold

30 stitches on hold

LEFT LEG

❹ RIGHT LEG IN PROGRESS

30 stitches cast on

30 stitches on hold

LOWER BACK

RUMP

RIGHT LEG

LEFT LEG

15 stitches on hold

❺ PREPARE TO WORK CROTCH

20 stitches picked up

20 stitches transferred

LOWER BACK

RUMP

10 stitches on hold

NEEDLE 3

NEEDLE 2

NEEDLE 1

15 stitches transferred

❻ PREPARE TO WORK BODY

55 stitches picked up

new beginning of round

10 stitches picked up

15 active stitches

10 stitches transferred

RIGHT LEG

CO 30 sts to end of left-hand needle, work to end—50 sts. Join for working in the rnd; pm for beginning of rnd.

Rnds 1–20: Knit (see Fig. 4).

Rnd 21: *K1, p1; repeat from * to end. Place markers every 10 sts to divide work into 5 sections.

Rnd 22 and 24: *Knit to 2 sts before marker, skp; repeat from * to end—35 sts remain after Rnd 24.

Rnd 23 and 25: *Skp, knit to marker; repeat from * to end—30 sts remain after Rnd 25.

Rnd 26: Knit.

Repeat Rnds 22–26 until 10 sts remain. Cut yarn, leaving an 8" tail. Thread tail through remaining sts, pull tight, and fasten off (see Fig. 5).

CROTCH

Transfer 20 sts from left-hand end of waste yarn at end of Left Leg to first dpn (Needle 1) (leaving 10 sts on waste yarn), 15 sts from waste yarn from Rump to second dpn (Needle 2),

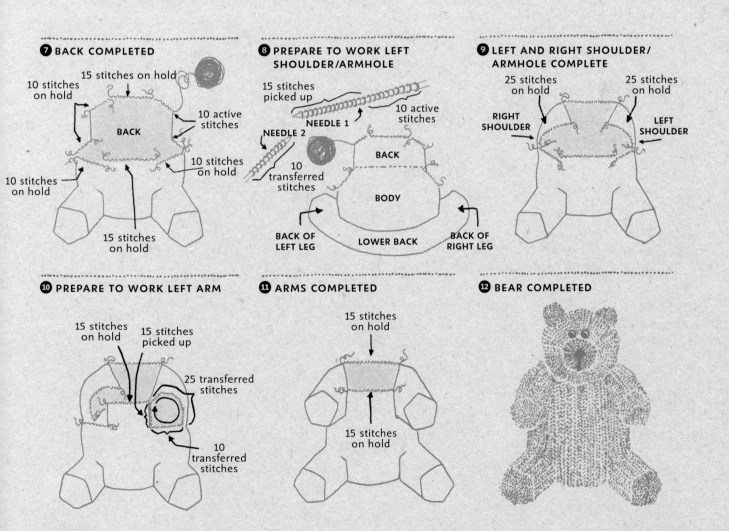

7 BACK COMPLETED

15 stitches on hold
10 stitches on hold
10 active stitches
BACK
10 stitches on hold
10 stitches on hold
15 stitches on hold

8 PREPARE TO WORK LEFT SHOULDER/ARMHOLE

15 stitches picked up
10 active stitches
NEEDLE 1
NEEDLE 2
10 transferred stitches
BACK
BODY
BACK OF LEFT LEG
LOWER BACK
BACK OF RIGHT LEG

9 LEFT AND RIGHT SHOULDER/ARMHOLE COMPLETE

25 stitches on hold
25 stitches on hold
RIGHT SHOULDER
LEFT SHOULDER

10 PREPARE TO WORK LEFT ARM

15 stitches on hold
15 stitches picked up
25 transferred stitches
10 transferred stitches

11 ARMS COMPLETED

15 stitches on hold
15 stitches on hold

12 BEAR COMPLETED

then pick up (but do not knit) 20 sts from CO edge of Right Leg with third dpn (Needle 3)—55 sts (see Fig. 5).

Row 1 (WS): Change to working back and forth. Transfer 1 st each from Needles 1 and 3 to Needle 2. With WS facing, join yarn to sts on Needle 2. P2tog-tbl, p13, p2tog; turn—53 sts remain.

Row 2: Transfer 1 st each from Needles 1 and 3 to Needle 2. K2tog, k13, ssk; turn—51 sts remain.

Row 3: Transfer 1 st each from Needles 1 and 3 to Needle 2. P2tog-tbl, p13, p2tog; turn—49 sts remain.

Rows 4–19: Repeat Rows 2 and 3—17 sts remain after Row 19.

Row 20: Repeat Row 2—15 sts remain.

BODY

Rnd 1: Change to working in the rnd. Pick up and knit 10 sts from top of Right Leg, pick up and knit 55 sts along Lower Back between Legs, pm for beginning of rnd, knit across 10 sts from waste yarn for Left Leg, knit across 15 sts from Crotch, knit to beginning of rnd—90 sts (see Fig. 6).

Rnds 2-4: Knit.

Note: Body is shaped using short rows (see page 156).

Rnd 5: K21, wrp-t; p7, wrp-t; k11, wrp-t; p15, wrp-t; k19, wrp-t, p23, wrp-t, knit to end, working wraps together with wrapped sts as you come to them.

Rnds 6–20: Knit.

BACK

Row 1: Knit to last 10 sts, turn.

Row 2: P35, turn. Transfer remaining 55 sts to five separate strands of waste yarn: 10 sts for Left Shoulder/Armhole, 10 sts for left underarm, 15 sts for Chest, 10 sts for right underarm, and 10 sts for Right Shoulder/Armhole.

Rows 3–14: Working on remaining 35 sts, work in St st.

Row 15: K35 and transfer 25 sts to two separate strands of waste yarn: First 10 sts for Right Shoulder and next 15 sts for Back neck—10 sts remain. Do not cut yarn. (see Fig. 7)

LEFT SHOULDER/ARMHOLE

Row 1 (RS): Transfer first 10 sts from waste yarn for Left Armhole to spare dpn or circ needle (Needle 2). With yarn attached to Needle 1, beginning at top of left armhole, pick up and knit 15 sts along left side edge of Back, turn—35 sts (25-10) (see Fig. 8).

Row 2: Transfer 1 st from Needle 2 to Needle 1. P2tog-tbl, purl to end—34 sts remain (25-9).

Row 3: Transfer 1 st from Needle 2 to Needle 1. Knit to last 2 sts on Needle 1, ssk—33 sts remain (25-8).

Repeat Rows 2 and 3 until all sts on Needle 2 have been worked—25 sts remain. Cut yarn and transfer sts to waste yarn for Left Arm (see Fig. 9).

RIGHT SHOULDER/ARMHOLE

Row 1 (RS): Transfer 10 sts from waste yarn for Right Armhole to spare dpn or circular needle (Needle 2). With Needle 1, beginning at bottom of right armhole, pick up and knit 15 sts along right side edge of Back, knit across 10 sts from waste yarn for Right Shoulder—35 sts (25-10).

Row 2: Transfer 1 st from Needle 2 to Needle 1. Purl to last 2 sts on Needle 1, p2tog—34 sts remain (25-9).

Row 3: Transfer 1 st from Needle 2 to Needle 1. K2tog, knit to end—33 sts remain (25-8).

Repeat Rows 2 and 3 until all sts on Needle 2 have been worked—25 sts remain. Cut yarn and transfer sts to waste yarn for Right Arm (see Fig. 9).

CHEST

Transfer 15 sts from waste yarn for Chest to dpn. With RS facing, join yarn. Begin St st; work even for 15 rows. Cut yarn and transfer sts to waste yarn for Head.

LEFT ARM

Knit across 25 sts from waste yarn for Left Arm, then across 10 sts from waste yarn for left underarm, then with spare dpn, pick up and knit 15 sts along edge of Chest—50 sts (see Fig. 10). Join for working in the rnd; pm for beginning of rnd. Knit 20 rnds. Complete as for Right Leg, beginning with Rnd 21.

RIGHT ARM

Knit across 25 sts from waste yarn for Right Arm, with spare dpn, pick up and knit 15 sts along edge of Chest, then knit across 10 sts from waste yarn for Right underarm—50 sts. Join for working in the rnd; pm for beginning of rnd. Knit 20 rnds. Complete as for Right Leg, beginning with Rnd 21 (see Fig. 11).

HEAD

Using Easy Circular CO or Disappearing Loop CO, CO 5 sts. Join for working in the rnd, being careful not to twist sts; pm for beginning of rnd. Work as for Rump until you have 75 sts, leaving sts on the needle(s).

Row 1 (WS): Change to working back and forth, removing beginning-of-rnd marker. Turn and purl to last 15 sts, transfer last 15 sts to waste yarn for Back neck.

Rows 2–9: Work in St st.

Rnd 1: Change to working in the rnd. Knit to end, knit across 15 sts from waste yarn from top of Chest; pm for beginning of rnd—75 sts.

Rnds 2–21: Knit.

FACE

Rnd 1: *K1, k2tog; repeat from * to end—50 sts remain.

Rnd 2: Knit.

Rnd 3: *K2tog; repeat from * to end—25 sts remain.

Rnds 4–8: Knit, removing beginning-of-rnd marker on last rnd.

Rnd 9: K1, *s2kp2 (creating a raised st), knit to 1 st before raised st; repeat from * until 5 sts remain. Cut yarn, leaving an 8" tail. Thread tail through remaining sts, pull tight, and fasten off.

EARS

CO 12 sts. Join for working in the rnd, being careful not to twist sts; pm for beginning of rnd.

Rnd 1: *K1-f/b, k1; repeat from * to end—18 sts.

Rnd 2: *K2, k1-f/b; repeat from * to end—24 sts.

Rnd 3: *K1-f/b, k3; repeat from * to end—30 sts.

Rnd 4: *K4, k1-f/b; repeat from * to end—36 sts.

Rnd 5: *K1-f/b, k5; repeat from * to end—42 sts.

Rnds 6–10: Knit.

Distribute sts evenly between 2 needles. Join sts using Three-Needle BO (see page 77).

FINISHING

With small amount of contrasting yarn and straight st, embroider nose (see photo). Sew eyes and ears in place (see photo and illustrations). Stuff Bear to desired firmness. Using Kitchener st (see page 154), join sts at base of Head and top of Back. Sew sides of Head to top of shoulders.

SHAWLS + BLANKETS

Revolutionary knitting is well suited for working a substantial project like a blanket or shawl. In creating the pieces that appear in this chapter, I drew my inspiration from the radially and rotationally symmetrical spiral shapes that occur throughout the natural world. You'll find shawls and blankets inspired by seashells and the roots and branches of trees, and in the shape of stars, seashells, spirals, and sunflowers.

FINISHED MEASUREMENTS
50" diameter

YARN
Woodstock Knits Luxe Cotton (100% organic cotton; 320 yards / 200 grams): 3 hanks Natural

NEEDLES
One set of four or five double-pointed needles (dpn) size US 10 (6 mm), and/or one or two 36" (90 cm) long or longer circular (circ) needles size US 10 (6 mm)

Change needle size if necessary to obtain correct gauge.

NOTIONS
Stitch markers (1 in color A for beginning of rnd; 15 in color B)

GAUGE
14 sts and 18 rows = 4" (10 cm) in Stockinette stitch (St st)

The traditional Shetland lace pattern Feather and Fan, or Old Shale, is intuitive and easy to remember. Each repeat of the pattern contains a hill of increases and a valley of decreases, separated by a few resting rounds of knits or purls. For this design, I've turned that traditional stitch pattern around, adding more and more increases and decreases into each successive ridge of the blanket. The resulting stitch pattern becomes ripplier and ripplier as the blanket grows. The wonderful texture of the doubled, thick-and-thin organic cotton yarn I chose for this project, combined with the airy openness of the stitch pattern, remind me of a field of Queen Anne's lace flowers in bloom.

STITCH PATTERNS

Ripple Pattern A

Note: You may work Ripple Pattern A from text or Chart.

(multiple of 3 sts at beginning; increases to 32 sts; 60 rnds)

Rnd 1: *[K1, yo] twice, k1; repeat from * to end—2 sts increased per repeat.

Rnd 2 and All Even-Numbered Rnds: Knit.

Rnd 3: Purl.

Rnd 5: *K2, yo, k1, yo, k2; repeat from * to end—2 sts increased per repeat.

Rnd 7: Purl.

Rnd 9: *K2tog, [yo, k1] 3 times, yo, ssk; repeat from * to end—2 sts increased per repeat.

Rnd 11: Purl..

Rnd 13: *K1, k2tog, [yo, k1] 3 times, yo, ssk, k1; repeat from * to end—2 sts increased per repeat.

Rnd 15: Purl.

Rnd 17: *K2, k2tog, [yo, k1] 3 times, yo, ssk, k2; repeat from * to end—2 sts increased per repeat

Rnd 19: Purl.

Rnd 21: *[K2tog] twice, [yo, k1] 5 times, yo, [ssk] twice; repeat from * to end—2 sts increased per repeat.

Rnd 23: Purl.

Rnd 25: *K1, [k2tog] twice, [yo, k1] 5 times, yo, [ssk] twice, k1; repeat from * to end—2 sts increased per repeat.

Rnd 27: Purl.

RIPPLE PATTERN A

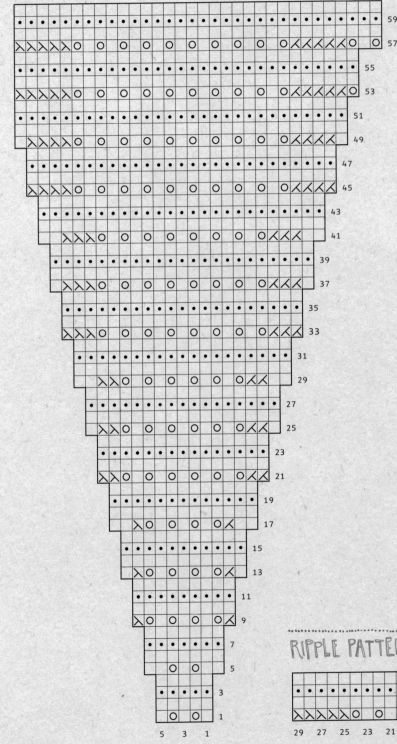

KEY

☐ Knit		⊙ Yo	⊠ Ssk
• Purl		⊠ K2tog	

RIPPLE PATTERN B

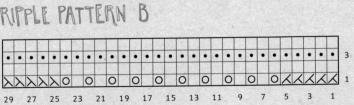

Rnd 29: *K2, [k2tog] twice, [yo, k1] 5 times, yo, [ssk] twice, k2; repeat from * to end—2 sts increased per repeat.

Rnd 31: Purl.

Rnd 33: *[K2tog] 3 times, [yo, k1] 7 times, yo, [ssk] 3 times; repeat from * to end—2 sts increased per repeat.

Rnd 35: Purl.

Rnd 37: *K1, [k2tog] 3 times, [yo, k1] 7 times, yo, [ssk] 3 times, k1; repeat from * to end—2 sts increased per repeat.

Rnd 39: Purl.

Rnd 41: *K2, [k2tog] 3 times, [yo, k1] 7 times, yo, [ssk] 3 times, k2; repeat from * to end—2 sts increased per repeat.

Rnd 43: Purl.

Rnd 45: *[K2tog] 4 times, [yo, k1] 9 times, yo, [ssk] 4 times; repeat from * to end—2 sts increased per repeat.

Rnd 47: Purl.

Rnd 49: *K1, [k2tog] 4 times, [yo, k1] 9 times, yo, [ssk] 4 times, k1; repeat from * to end—2 sts increased per repeat.

Rnd 51: Purl.

Rnd 53: *Yo, [k2tog] 5 times, [yo, k1] 9 times, yo, [ssk] 5 times; repeat from * to end—1 st increased per repeat.

Rnd 55: Purl.

Rnd 57: *Yo, k1, yo, [k2tog] 5 times, [yo, k1] 9 times, yo, [ssk] 5 times; repeat from * to end—2 sts increased per repeat.

Rnd 59: Purl.

Ripple Pattern B

Note: You may work Ripple Pattern B from text or Chart.

(panel of 29 sts; 4-rnd repeat)

Rnd 1: [K2tog] 5 times, [yo, k1] 9 times, yo, [ssk] 5 times.

Rnd 2: Knit.

Rnd 3: Purl.

Rnd 4: Knit.

Repeat Rnds 1–4 for Ripple Pattern B.

BLANKET

Using Easy Circular CO (see page 144) or Disappearing Loop CO (see page 148), CO 8 sts. Divide sts among 2 or more needles if necessary for your preferred method of working in the rnd. Join for working in the rnd, being careful not to twist sts; pm (color A) for beginning of rnd. Purl 1 rnd. Knit 1 rnd.

First Set of Ripples

Setup Rnd: *[K1, yo, k1] in same st; repeat from * to end—24 sts. Place 7 additional markers (color B) every 3 sts. Knit 1 rnd.

Next Rnd: Begin Ripple Pattern A. *Note: You may work pattern from text or Chart. Change to circ needle(s) if necessary for number of sts on needle(s). Work even until Ripple Pattern A is complete—256 sts (32 sts between markers). Place marker (color B) 3 sts after each existing marker (8 additional markers placed).*

Second Set of Ripples

Next Rnd: *Work Ripple Pattern A to next marker, slip marker, work Ripple Pattern B to next marker, slip marker; repeat from * to end. Work even through Rnd 50 of Ripple Pattern A—464 sts (29 sts between markers). Purl 3 rnds. BO all sts loosely.

FINISHING

Block as desired.

dahlia blanket

The design of this blanket was the result of a happy experiment. Barbara Walker's epic *Treasury of Knitting Patterns* contains a fascinating and beautiful herringbone stitch called Dragon Skin, in which an intuitive combination of increases and decreases creates a scalloped-looking fabric. I wondered what would happen if I adapted that pattern to revolutionary knitting, and was surprised to find the floral shape of this blanket on my needles. Like the dahlia for which it is named, each successive ring of petals in this blanket is larger than the last. The raised stitches that define the edges of the "petals" are made by decreasing at the same point in each round. These ridges zigzag back and forth as the blanket grows, before dissolving into a sea of seed stitch. The outstanding stitch definition of the yarn I chose and the intuitiveness of the zigzag pattern make this a good project for learning to read your knitting.

FINISHED MEASUREMENTS
38" diameter

YARN
Blue Sky Alpacas Worsted Hand Dyes (50% royal alpaca / 50% merino; 100 yards / 100 grams): 8 hanks #2008 Light Pink

NEEDLES
One set of four or five double-pointed needles (dpn) size US 9 (5.5 mm), and/or one or two 36" (90 cm) long circular (circ) needle(s) size US 9 (5.5 mm)

Change needle size if necessary to obtain correct gauge.

NOTIONS
23 stitch markers (1 in color A for beginning of round, 11 each in colors B and C)

GAUGE
18 sts and 24 rows = 4" (10 cm) in Stockinette stitch (St st)

BLANKET

Using Easy Circular CO (see page 144) or Disappearing Loop CO (see page 148), CO 11 sts. Divide sts among 2 or more needles if necessary for your preferred method of working in the rnd. Join for working in the rnd, being careful not to twist sts; pm (color A) for beginning of rnd.

Rnd 1: *Yo, k1; repeat from * to end—22 sts.

Rnd 2: *Yo, k2tog; repeat from * to end.

Rnd 3: *Yo, k2; repeat from * to end—33 sts.

Rnd 4: *Yo, ssk, k1; repeat from * to end.

Rnd 5: *Yo, k3; repeat from * to end—44 sts.

Rnd 6: *Yo, k2, ssk; repeat from * to end.

Rnd 7: *K4, yo; repeat from * to end—55 sts.

Rnd 8: *K2, k2tog, k1, yo; repeat from * to end.

Rnd 9: *K5, yo; repeat from * to end—66 sts.

Rnd 10: *K1, k2tog, k3, yo; repeat from * to end.

Rnd 11: *K6, yo; repeat from * to end—77 sts.

Rnd 12: *K2tog, k5, yo; repeat from * to end.

Partial Rnd: Remove beginning-of-rnd marker, k7, pm (color A) for new beginning of rnd. Place 11 additional markers (color B) every 7 sts. *Note: You will have 2 markers at beginning of rnd, 1 of each color.*

FIRST PETAL RING

Rnd 1: *Yo, knit to marker, sm; repeat from * to end—88 sts (8 sts each section).

Rnd 2: *Yo, k1, ssk, knit to marker, sm; repeat from * to end.

Rnd 3: Repeat Rnd 1—99 sts (9 sts in each section).

Rnd 4: *Yo, knit to raised st (ssk from 2 rnds before), ssk, knit to marker, sm; repeat from * to end.

Repeat Rnds 3 and 4 until ssk has been worked on last 2 sts of each section—143 sts (13 sts in each section).

Partial Rnd: Remove beginning-of-rnd marker (leaving other markers in place), knit to next marker, pm (color A) for new beginning of rnd.

SECOND PETAL RING

Rnd 1: *Knit to marker, yo, sm; repeat from * to end—154 sts (14 sts in each section).

Rnd 2: *Knit to 3 sts before marker, k2tog, k1, yo, sm; repeat from * to end.

Rnd 3: Repeat Rnd 1—165 sts (15 sts in each section).

Rnd 4: *Knit to 1 st before raised st (k2tog from 2 rnds before), k2tog, knit to marker, yo, sm; repeat from * to end.

Repeat Rnds 3 and 4 until k2tog has been worked on first 2 sts of each section—275 sts (25 sts in each section).

FINAL PETAL RING

Rnd 1: *Knit to 1 st before marker, pm (color C), k1-f/b, sm; repeat from * to end—286 sts (26 sts in each section).

Rnd 2: *Ssk, knit to color C marker, sm, k1-f/b, k1; repeat from * to end.

Rnd 3: *Knit to color C marker, sm, k1-f/b, **k1, p1; repeat from ** to color B marker; repeat from * to end—297 sts (27 sts in each section).

Rnd 4: *Ssk, knit to color C marker, sm, k1-f/b, knit the purl sts and purl the knit sts to color B marker; repeat from * to end.

Repeat Rnds 3 and 4 until there is only 1 st between beginning of each section and color C marker—528 sts (46 sts in each section).

BO all sts in pattern.

YARN
The Fibre Company Road to China
Light (65% baby alpaca / 15% silk /
10% camel / 10% cashmere; 159
yards / 50 grams): 10 hanks Citrine

NEEDLES
One set of four or five double-
pointed needles (dpn) size US 6
(4 mm), and/or one or two 36"
(90 cm) long or longer circular
(circ) needle(s) size US 6 (4 mm)

Change needle size if necessary to
obtain correct gauge.

NOTIONS
43 stitch markers in 4 different
colors (1 in color A for beginning
of rnd; 13 in color B; 8 in color C;
21 in color D); 21 safety pins

GAUGE
20 sts and 28 rows = 4" (10 cm)
in Stockinette stitch (St st), before
blocking

sunflower shawl

If you look closely at the bracts of a pinecone, the seeds in a dried sunflower head, or the skin of a pineapple, you'll see a pattern of right-slanting and left-slanting spirals intersecting. And to make this phenomenon of the natural world even more interesting, you'll usually find a pair of consecutive Fibonacci numbers in the mix. For example, a sunflower head may have 34 right-slanting spirals followed by 55 left-slanting spirals. Fibonacci numbers are a series of numbers in which each new number is found by adding the previous two together: 0, 1, 1, 2, 3, 5, 8, 13, 21, etc. (see page 100).

In designing and making this shawl, I wanted to use my knitting to celebrate this natural pattern. As you work it outward from the center, a thirteen-spoke spiral arcs to the right while an eight-spoke spiral travels left. These arcs cross as the shawl grows outward, forming the sunflower motif. Finally, the petals come to points as a lace border gradually grows between each one.

STITCH PATTERN

Lace Pattern (multiples vary; 8-rnd repeat)
Note: You may work Lace Pattern from text or Chart.
Rnd 1: [Yo] twice.
Rnd 2: [K1, k1-tbl] into double yo.
Rnd 3: Yo, k2, yo.
Rnd 4: K4.
Rnd 5: [Yo] twice, ssk, k2tog, [yo] twice.
Rnds 6, 8, 10, and 12: Knit, working [k1, k1-tbl] into double yo.
Rnd 7: Yo, k1, *k2tog, [yo] twice, ssk; repeat from * to last st, k1, yo.
Rnd 9: Yo, *k2tog, [yo] twice, ssk; repeat from * to end, yo.
Rnd 11: Yo, k1, yo, ssk, *k2tog, [yo] twice, ssk; repeat from * to last 3 sts, k2tog, yo, k1, yo.
Rnd 13: [Yo] twice, ssk, *k2tog, [yo] twice, ssk; repeat from * to last 2 sts, k2tog, [yo] twice.
Rnd 14: Repeat Rnd 6.
Repeat Rnds 7–14 for Lace Pattern.

NOTES

As complicated as this design may look, the pattern repeat is only five rounds long, with special instructions on what to do when the paths of the spiral arcs cross. Writing it out stitch by stitch would take dozens of pages, and would be no fun at all to follow, so I wrote general rules to guide you instead. I'm sure you'll find that they're nearly intuitive once you get going.

When working the Body of this Shawl, you will find a series of rules following each round for subsequent repeats of that round. Look at the location of the markers mentioned in the rules to determine which rule applies to your current repeat of the round. Apply that rule as you repeat the round, working the original round instructions and whatever modifications are required by the appropriate rule. The rules are based on the location and manipulation of the different stitch markers, so be sure to use different color (or style) markers as indicated, and place the markers as instructed under Body.

SHAWL

Using Easy Circular CO (see page 144) or Disappearing Loop CO (see page 148), and Magic Loop Method (see page 152), CO 13 sts. Divide sts among 2 or more needles if necessary for your prefered method of working in the rnd. Join for working in the rnd, being careful not to twist sts; pm (color A) for beginning of rnd.

Rnds 1 and 2: Knit.

Rnd 3: *Yo, k1; repeat from * to end— 26 sts.

Rnds 4 and 5: *Yo, k2tog; repeat from * to end.

Rnd 6: *Yo, k2; repeat from * to end— 39 sts.

Rnds 7 and 8: *Yo, k1, k2tog; repeat from * to end.

Rnd 9: *Yo, k3; repeat from * to end— 52 sts.

Rnds 10 and 11: *Yo, k2, k2tog; repeat from * to end.

BODY

Place color B markers every 4 sts (13 additional markers placed) and color C markers [every 6 sts, then every 7 sts] 4 times (8 additional markers placed). You will have markers B and C together after 32 sts, and markers A, B, and C together at the beginning of the rnd.

Work Rnds 1–5 below once, then repeat Rnds 1–5, following the rules given below each Rnd (see Notes), until Shawl measures 18" from the center.

Rnd 1 (Increase Rnd): Knit, working yo

CREATING SUNFLOWER MOTIF

❶ 13 RIGHT-SLANTING SECTIONS (BODY RNDS 2 AND 4)

❷ 8 LEFT-SLANTING SECTIONS (BODY RNDS 3 AND 5)

❸ LEFT-SLANTING AND RIGHT-SLANTING SECTIONS COMBINED

after every B marker and before every C marker.

On following repeats of Rnd 1, the following rules apply:

- If the rnd just worked ended with a yo and the upcoming rnd is supposed to begin with another yo, work M1 instead of the yo at beginning of rnd.

- If markers B and C are together, sm B, yo, then sm C.

- If markers B and A are together, sm B, yo, then sm A.

- If markers C and A are together, sm A, yo, then sm C.

- If markers B, C, and A are together, sm B, yo, sm A, then sm C.

Rnds 2 and 4 (Right-Slanting Spiral): *Knit to 2 sts before marker B, k2tog, sm B, yo; repeat from * to last marker B, knit to end.

On following repeats of Rnds 2 and 4, the following rules apply:

- If a marker C is between the 2 sts to be worked in the k2tog, remove marker C, k2tog, sm B, yo, replace marker C.

- If rnd begins with only 1 st between marker A and first marker B, remove marker A, k1, slip marker B, replace marker A, then work Rnd as instructed above.

- If markers B and A are together, sm B, yo, sm A.

- If markers B and C are together, sm B, yo, sm C.

Rnds 3 and 5 (Left-Slanting Spiral): Knit to first marker C, yo, sm C, *ssk, knit to next marker C, yo, sm C; repeat from * to last marker C, ssk, knit to end.

On following repeats of Rnds 3 and 5, the following rules apply:

- If first marker C is at beginning of rnd, omit "Knit to first marker C" from instructions, and begin with "yo, sm C".

- If a marker B is between the 2 sts to be worked in the ssk, remove marker B and replace it 1 st to the right and to the right of the marker C, ssk.

- If markers B and C are together, sm B, yo, sm C.

- If only 1 st remains between final marker C and marker A, move marker A 1 st to the right and to the right of marker C, ssk, then continue with next rnd.

BORDER

Partial Rnd: Remove marker A, knit to first marker (either B or C), replace marker A for new beginning of rnd, leaving all other markers in place.

Work is now divided into 21 sections separated by markers B and C. Count sts in each section between markers and place a safety pin in the center of all sections that contain a multiple of 4 sts. Ignore marker A when counting section sts.

Transition Rnd: *In all pinned sections, yo, knit to 2 sts before marker, k2tog, sm; in all non-pinned sections, yo, knit to marker; repeat from * to end—1 st increased per non-pinned section. Re-count non-pinned sections; place pins on all sections that now contain a multiple of 4 sts.

Repeat Transition Rnd until all sections are pinned. Each section will contain a multiple of 4 sts. *Note: This transition will likely require 3 rnds, but may require fewer depending on the st count in each section.*

FROM FIBONACCI TO PHI

Taking their name from the nickname of the thirteenth-century mathematician Leonardo of Pisa, whose book Liber Abaci ("the book of computation") convinced Europe to adopt the Arabic numerals we use today, Fibonacci numbers are a series where each new number is found by adding the previous two together—0, 1, 1, 2, 3, 5, 8, 13, 21, 34, 55, 89 . . . and so on. Pretty simple so far, right?

It turns out that this simple series of numbers is a set of nature's magic numbers. For example, if you count the petals of many flowers, you'll find a Fibonacci number.

If you draw a series of squares with their sides one Fibonacci number long, they'll fit together as shown. Drawing a curve to connect the corners of those squares will produce the Golden Spiral, a seashell-like shape. This shape is found throughout the natural world, everywhere from the path of a moth approaching a candle to the spiral arms of our galaxy.

You can see that adding each larger square to the series creates a rectangle, and that the rectangles created this way have similar overall proportions. The rectangle created this way is referred to as the Golden Rectangle. You can find Golden Rectangles throughout the human-made world, from the rectangular United Nations building in New York City to the familiar shapes of photographs and computer screens.

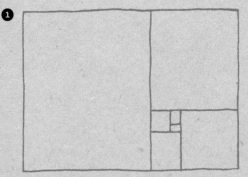

Fibonacci Squares from the Golden Rectangle

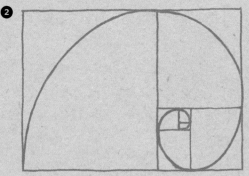

The Golden Spiral

Dividing the length of the long side of the rectangle by the short side, or simply dividing one Fibonacci number by the previous one in the set, is a way of finding of the Golden Mean, or ϕ (phi), approximately 1.61. Like π, this number is a ratio, and this ratio is found throughout nature. For example, if you measure the distance from your elbow to wrist, then your wrist to fingertips, you'll likely find the first measurement is about 1.6 times as long as the second. You can find the same ratio repeated in many places throughout the human body, for example the chin to the brow to the top of the head, or the top of the head to the navel to the toes.

PETALS

Partial Rnd: Count sts and locate and mark center point of widest section. If multiple sections have the same number of sts as the widest section, mark the first one you come to. Remove marker A, knit to marked center point, replace marker A for new beginning of rnd.

Note: You may work Lace Pattern from text or Chart.

Rnd 1: Knit to first marker (either B or C), *sm, work Lace Pattern, pm (color D), knit to next marker; repeat from * to end.

Rnds 2–4: Knit to marker, *sm, work Lace Pattern to marker, sm, knit to marker; repeat from * to end.

Rnd 5: *Knit to 2 sts before marker, k2tog, sm, work Lace Pattern to marker, sm, ssk; repeat from * through last marker (the marker before marker A), knit to end.

Rnd 6: Repeat Rnd 2. Remove markers from both sides of any sections containing only 4 sts.

Rnds 7, 9, 11, and 13: Repeat Rnd 5.

Rnds 8, 10, 12, and 14: Knit to marker, *sm, work Lace Pattern to marker, sm, knit to marker; repeat from * to end. Remove markers from both sides of any sections containing only 4 sts.

Repeat Rnds 7–14 until only 1 st remains between marker A and next marker.

BO Rnd: K1, *yo, k1, pass first st and yo together over last st; repeat from * until all sts are BO.

FINISHING

Soak Shawl and lay flat. Pin Petals where they intersect and where they reach the BO edge, then stretch and pin lace sections as desired between Petals. Allow to air dry.

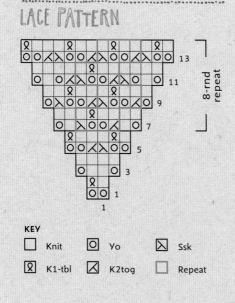

LACE PATTERN

8-rnd repeat

13
11
9
7
5
3
1

1

KEY

☐ Knit	⊙ Yo	⊠ Ssk
⊠ K1-tbl	⊠ K2tog	☐ Repeat

isosceles shawl

In geometry, a triangle with two sides of equal length is called isosceles, while a triangle whose sides are each a different length is called scalene. The challenge I set for myself in designing this piece was to create a triangular shawl shape that begins in the center. Working yarnover increases at three regular points divides the work into three triangles. You can see that the large triangle that forms the long edge of this shawl is an isosceles triangle, while the two smaller triangles that make the shorter edges are scalene. I love how the three triangles come together, giving the shawl its overall isosceles triangle shape.

SHAWL

Using Easy Circular CO (see page 144) or Disappearing Loop CO (see page 148), CO 15 sts. Divide sts among 2 or more needles if necessary for your preferred method of working in the rnd. Join for working in the rnd, being careful not to twist sts; pm for beginning of rnd.

Rnds 1 and 2: Knit.

Rnd 3: *Yo, k1, yo, k4; repeat from * to end—21 sts.

Rnd 4: Knit, placing removable markers on sts 2, 9, and 16; this will divide work into four sections (1-7-7-6) sts. Move markers up as you go. *Note: In section counts, the marked st will be counted with the sts that follow it.*

Rnd 5: [K1, yo] twice, k6, [yo, k1] twice, yo, k4, [yo, k1] twice, yo, k5—29 sts (2-9-11-7 sts); 1-2-4-1 sts increased.

Rnd 6: Knit.

Body

Rnd 7: *Knit to marked st, yo, k1, yo; repeat from * twice, knit to end—35 sts (3-11-13-8 sts; 1-2-2-1 sts increased).

Rnd 8: Knit to second marked st, k1, *yo, k2tog, yo, ssk; repeat from * to third marked st, knit to end.

Rnd 9: [Knit to marked st, yo, k1, yo] twice, k1, yo, knit to 1 st before next marked st, [yo, k1] twice, yo, knit to end—43 sts (4-13-17-9 sts; 1-2-4-1 sts increased).

FINISHED MEASUREMENTS

Approximately 55" wide at widest point x 39" tall

YARN

ShiBui Knits Silk Cloud (60% kid mohair / 40% silk; 330 yards / 25 grams): 2 hanks Graphite

NEEDLES

One set of four or five double-pointed needles (dpn) size US 6 (4 mm), and/or one or two 36" (90 cm) long or longer circular (circ) needle(s), size US 6 (4 mm)

Change needle size if necessary to obtain correct gauge.

NOTIONS

Stitch marker; 3 removable markers or safety pins

GAUGE

13 sts and 32 rows = 4" (10 cm) in Stockinette st (St st)

LACE BORDER

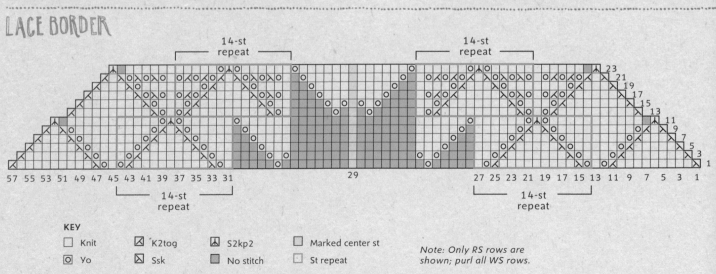

KEY

- ☐ Knit
- ⊙ Yo
- ⊠ K2tog
- ⊠ Ssk
- ⋏ S2kp2
- ▨ No stitch
- ☐ Marked center st
- ⫶ St repeat

Note: Only RS rows are shown; purl all WS rows.

Rnds 10 and 12: Knit.

Rnd 11: Repeat Rnd 7—49 sts (5-15-19-10 sts; 1-2-2-1 sts increased).

Rnd 13: Repeat Rnd 9—57 sts (6-17-23-11 sts; 1-2-4-1 sts increased).

Rnd 14: Knit.

Note: Change to circ needle(s) if necessary for number of sts on needle(s).

Repeat Rnds 7–10 twenty-four times, increasing 14 sts (2-4-6-2) with each repeat—393 sts (54-113-167-59 sts).

Partial BO Rnd: Remove beginning-of-rnd marker, knit to second marked st, BO all sts knitwise through third marked st, removing markers on sts as you BO—225 sts remain (112-113). The long side of the triangle has now been BO.

Lace Border

Note: You may work Lace Border from text or Chart.

Row 1: Ssk, k9, k2tog, yo, k1, *yo, ssk, k9, k2tog, yo, k1; repeat from * to marked st, yo, k1, yo, **k1, yo, ssk, k9, k2tog, yo; repeat from ** to last 14 sts, k1, yo, ssk, k9, k2tog.

Row 2 and all WS Rows: Purl.

Row 3: Ssk, k7, k2tog, yo, k2, *k1, yo, ssk, k7, k2tog, yo, k2; repeat from * to 1 st before marked st, [yo, k1] 3 times, yo, **k2, yo, ssk, k7, k2tog, yo, k1; repeat from ** to last 13 sts, k2, yo, ssk, k7, k2tog.

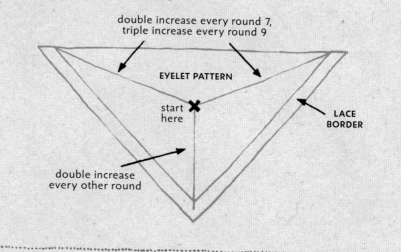

ANATOMY OF ISOCELES SHAWL

double increase every round 7, triple increase every round 9

EYELET PATTERN

start here

LACE BORDER

double increase every other round

Row 5: Ssk, k5, k2tog, yo, k3, *k2, yo, ssk, k5, k2tog, yo, k3; repeat from * to 3 sts before marked st, yo, k7, yo, **k3, yo, ssk, k5, k2tog, yo, k2; repeat from ** to last 12 sts, k3, yo, ssk, k5, k2tog.

Row 7: Ssk, k3, k2tog, yo, k4, *k3, yo, ssk, k3, k2tog, yo, k4; repeat from * to 4 sts before marked st, yo, k9, yo, **k4, yo, ssk, k3, k2tog, yo, k3; repeat from ** to last 11 sts, k4, yo, ssk, k3, k2tog.

Row 9: Ssk, k1, k2tog, yo, k5, *k4, yo, ssk, k1, k2tog, yo, k5; repeat from * to 5 sts before marked st, yo, k11, yo, **k5, yo, ssk, k1, k2tog, yo, k4; repeat from ** to last 10 sts, k5, yo, ssk, k1, k2tog.

Row 11: S2kp2, k6, *k5, yo, s2kp2, yo, k6; repeat from * to 6 sts before marked st, yo, k13, yo, **k6, yo, s2kp2, yo, k5; repeat from ** to last 9 sts, k6, s2kp2.

Row 13: Repeat Row 1.

Row 15: Repeat Row 3.

Row 17: Ssk, k5, [k2tog, yo] twice, k1, *[yo, ssk] twice, k5, [k2tog, yo] twice, k1; repeat from * to 3 sts before marked st, yo, k7, yo, **k1, [yo, ssk] twice, k5, [k2tog, yo] twice; repeat from ** to last 12 sts, k1, [yo, ssk] twice, k5, k2tog.

Row 19: Repeat Row 7.

Row 21: Ssk, k1, [k2tog, yo] 3 times, k1, *[yo, ssk] 3 times, k1, [k2tog, yo] 3 times, k1; repeat from * to 5 sts before marked st, yo, k11, yo, **k1, [yo, ssk] 3 times, k1, [k2tog, yo] 3 times; repeat from ** to last 10 sts, k1, [yo, ssk] 3 times, k1, k2tog.

Row 23: Repeat Row 11.

Row 24: Purl. BO all sts knitwise.

FINISHED MEASUREMENTS
Approximately 85" wide at bind-off edge x 15" long

YARN
Louet Euroflax Sport Weight (100% wet spun linen; 270 yards / 100 grams): 2 hanks #58 Burgundy

NEEDLES
One 36" (90 cm) long or longer circular (circ) needle size US 6 (4 mm)

Change needle size if necessary to obtain correct gauge.

NOTIONS
Stitch markers

GAUGE
18 sts and 25 rows = 4" (10 cm) in Stockinette stitch (St st)

spiral petal shawl

In most of the patterns in this chapter, you create flat fabric by increasing at regular points in each revolution, like the four corners of the Tree of Life Afghan on page 119. As I designed these projects, I began to wonder what would happen if I put together all the increases needed for each round. The answer: a spiral.

In this shawl, you work eight increases together while working a lace pattern. You begin each set of increases where the last one ended, creating a line of yarnovers that travels upward and to the left across the fabric. This increase pattern gives the shawl its circular shape, while the distinctive line of yarnovers forms the spiral that swirls through the lace petals.

STITCH PATTERN

Chevron Pattern (multiple of 8 sts; 10-row repeat)
Note: You may work Chevron Pattern from text or Chart.
Rows 1 and 3 (RS): *K1, ssk, k1, [yo, k1] twice, k2tog; repeat from * to end.
Row 2 and All WS Rows: Purl.
Row 5: *K1, yo, ssk, k3, k2tog, yo; repeat from * to end.
Row 7: *K2, yo, ssk, k1, k2tog, yo, k1; repeat from * to end.
Row 9: *K3, yo, s2kp2, yo, k2; repeat from * to end.
Row 10: Purl.
Repeat Rows 1–10 for Chevron Pattern.

NOTES

In this pattern, you will modify a chevron lace motif by doubling the stitch count of one repeat of the pattern on every RS row (8 sts increased per RS row). The spiral shape of the shawl will emerge as you place each successive row of increases to the left of the previous one.

In each row, the marker indicating where to begin working the increases moves one section (8 stitches) to the left. When you no longer have enough stitches to move the marker one section to the left, you will remove it and replace it where indicated the next time you repeat Row 1 of the pattern. The next Wave of the spiral will then continue from right to left.

CHEVRON PATTERN

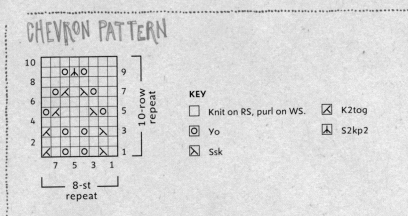

KEY

□ Knit on RS, purl on WS.		⊠ K2tog
O Yo		⅄ S2kp2
⊠ Ssk		

SHAWL

First Wave

CO 47 sts.

Row 1 (RS): Slip 1, k2, [k1, yo] 8 times, pm, k8, work in Chevron Pattern to last 4 sts, k4—55 sts.

Row 2 and All WS Rows Throughout: Slip 1, purl to end.

Rows 3 and 5: Slip 1, k2, work in Chevron Pattern to marker, remove marker, [k1, yo] 8 times, pm, k8, work in Chevron Pattern to last 4 sts, k4—71 sts after Row 5.

Row 7: Slip 1, k2, work in Chevron Pattern to marker, remove marker, [k1, yo] 8 times, pm, k12—79 sts.

Row 9: Slip 1, k2, work in Chevron Pattern to marker, remove marker, [k1, yo] 8 times, k4—87 sts.

Row 11: Slip 1, k10, work in Chevron Pattern to last 4 sts, k4.

Second Wave

Row 1: Repeat Row 1 of First Wave—95 sts.

Row 3 and All RS Rows Through 15: Repeat Row 3 of First Wave—151 sts after Row 15.

Row 17: Repeat Row 7 of First Wave—159 sts.

Row 19: Repeat Row 9 of First Wave—167 sts.

Row 21: Repeat Row 11 of First Wave.

Third Wave

Row 1: Repeat Row 1 of First Wave—175 sts.

Row 3 and All RS Rows Through 35: Repeat Row 3—311 sts after Row 35.

FINISHED SHAWL

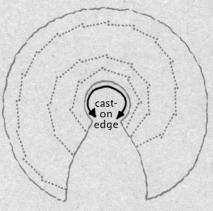

Yarnover increases form a spiral pattern around the shawl.

Row 37: Repeat Row 7 of First Wave—319 sts.

Row 39: Repeat Row 9 of First Wave—327 sts.

Row 41: Repeat Row 11 of First Wave—335 sts.

Row 43: Slip 1, k6, *[k1-yo-k1] in same st, k7; repeat from * to end—417 sts.

Row 45: Knit.

Row 46: Purl.

BO all sts knitwise.

FINISHING
Block as desired.

VARIATIONS

The underlying structure of this shawl—increasing by 8 stitches every other row, and starting each batch of increases to the left of where the last one ended—will work with many stitch patterns. You might want to experiment with a different lace motif. Or you could change the pattern of increases. In most cases, as long as the number of increases averages 4 per row, the work will lay flat. For example, 4 increases in every row or 16 increases every fourth row will give the same result—and an airy lace pattern makes it easier for the fabric to lie down as well. Remember that variations will also affect the yarn requirements.

feather and fan shawl

This shawl combines two traditional elements—a Faroese-inspired shape and the Feather and Fan lace pattern. Faroese shawls are distinguished by their bat-wing shape, with shoulder shaping worked on either side of a gusset that runs vertically down the back. In this version, you divide the work into eleven sections. The five sections on either end start with just a few stitches and grow wider in successive rows, while you work the center panel "as is," always maintaining the same number of stitches. The result is a "Pac-Man" shape, as the two sides become half circles that drape over the shoulders. To make it easier to read your knitting, I've separated each panel with a purl stitch.

STITCH PATTERNS

Feather and Fan Pattern (for gauge swatch)
(multiple of 17 sts; 4-row repeat)
Row 1 (RS): [K2tog] 3 times, [yo, k1] 5 times, yo, [ssk] 3 times.
Row 2: Purl.
Row 3: Knit.
Row 4: Purl.
Repeat Rows 1–4 for Feather and Fan Pattern.

Lace Pattern
(panel of 3 sts at CO, increases to panel of 39 sts; 2 sts increased per increase row)
Note: You may work Lace Pattern from text or Chart.
Row 1 (RS): [K1, yo] twice, k1.
Rows 2–4: Work in St st.
Row 5: K2, yo, k1, yo, k2.
Rows 6–8: Work in St st.
Row 9: K2tog, [yo, k1] 3 times, yo, ssk.
Rows 10–12: Work in St st.
Row 13: K2tog, [k1, yo], 4 times, k1, ssk.
Rows 14–16: Work in St st.
Row 17: K2tog, k2, [yo, k1] 3 times, yo, k2, ssk.
Rows 18–20: Work in St st.
Row 21: [K2tog] twice, [yo, k1] 5 times, yo, [ssk] twice.
Rows 22–24: Work in St st.

FINISHED MEASUREMENTS
Approximately 16 1/4" wide at CO edge x 17" long; approximately 90 1/2" wide at end of Body, before working Edging

YARN
ShiBui Knits Heichi (100% silk; 105 yards / 50 grams): 7 hanks #H71 Column

NEEDLES
One 24" (60 cm) long or longer circular (circ) needle, size US 9 (5.5 mm)

Change needle size if necessary to obtain correct gauge.

GAUGE
16 sts and 20 rows = 4" (10 cm) in Feather and Fan Pattern

Row 25: [K2tog] twice, [k1, yo] 6 times, k1, [ssk] twice.

Rows 26–28: Work in St st.

Row 29: [K2tog] twice, k2, [yo, k1] 5 times, yo, k2, [ssk] twice.

Rows 30–32: Work in St st.

Row 33: [K2tog] 3 times, [yo, k1] 7 times, yo, [ssk] 3 times.

Rows 34–36: Work in St st.

Row 37: [K2tog] 3 times, [k1, yo] 8 times, k1, [ssk] 3 times.

Rows 38–40: Work in St st.

Row 41: [K2tog] 3 times, k2, [yo, k1] 7 times, yo, k2, [ssk] 3 times.

Rows 42–44: Work in St st.

Row 45: [K2tog] 4 times, [yo, k1] 9 times, yo, [ssk] 4 times.

Rows 46–48: Work in St st.

Row 49: [K2tog] 4 times, [k1, yo] 10 times, k1, [ssk] 4 times.

Rows 50–52: Work in St st.

Row 53: [K2tog] 4 times, k2, [yo, k1] 9 times, yo, k2, [ssk] 4 times.

Rows 54–56: Work in St st.

Row 57: [K2tog] 5 times, [yo, k1] 11 times, yo, [ssk] 5 times.

Rows 58–60: Work in St st.

Row 61: [K2tog] 5 times, [k1, yo] 12 times, k1, [ssk] 5 times.

Rows 62–64: Work in St st.

Row 65: [K2tog] 5 times, k2, [yo, k1] 11 times, yo, k2, [ssk] 5 times.

Rows 66–68: Work in St st.

Row 69: [K2tog] 6 times, [yo, k1] 13 times, yo, [ssk] 6 times.

Rows 70–72: Work in St st.

LACE PATTERN

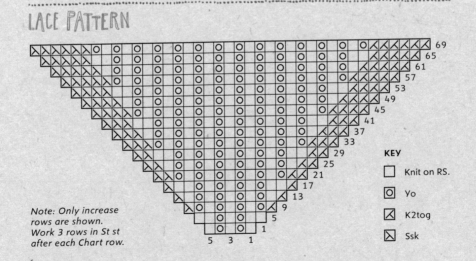

Note: Only increase rows are shown. Work 3 rows in St st after each Chart row.

KEY

☐ Knit on RS.

⊡ Yo

⧄ K2tog

⧅ Ssk

BODY

CO 65 sts.

Setup Row (WS): Slip 1, p2, [k1, p3] 5 times, k1, p17, [k1, p3] 6 times.

Row 1: Slip 1, k2, p1, [work Lace Pattern from text or Chart, p1] 5 times, [k2tog] 3 times, [yo, k1] 5 times, yo, [ssk] 3 times, [p1, work Lace Pattern from text or Chart] 5 times, p1, k3.

Rows 2–4: Slip 1, knit the knit sts and purl the purl sts as they face you, purl all yos.

Repeat Rows 1–4 until Lace Pattern has been completed (you should have 73 rows total)—425 sts (piece will measure approximately 14" from the beginning).

EDGING

Row 1 (RS): Slip 1, k2, *yo, k1; repeat from * to last 3 sts, k3—844 sts.

Row 2: Slip 1, purl to end.

Row 3: Slip 1, knit to end.

Row 4: Repeat Row 2.

BO Row: K1, *yo, k1, pass first st and yo together over last st; repeat from * until all sts are BO.

FINISHING

Block as desired.

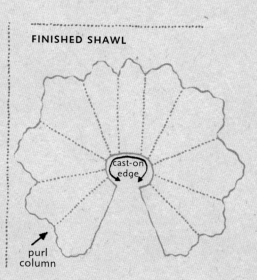

FINISHED SHAWL

cast-on edge

purl column

star baby blanket/ play mat

This thick and squooshy corrugated star can be used as either a blanket or a play mat. You begin in the center by making a pentagon, incorporating the pattern of increase stitches into the ribbing as the blanket grows. After the pentagon has reached the size you like, you form the first point of the star by working one side of the pentagon back and forth, decreasing at one end of every row until the rib comes together into a point. You then repeat this process on the four remaining sides. A star is born!

STITCH PATTERN

2x2 Rib (for gauge swatch)
(multiple of 4 sts; 1-row repeat)
Row 1 (RS): *K2, p2; repeat from * to end.
Row 2: Knit the knit sts and purl the purl sts as they face you.
Repeat Row 2 for 2x2 Rib.

BLANKET

Using Easy Circular CO (see page 144) or Disappearing Loop CO (see page 148), CO 5 sts. Divide sts among 2 or more needles if necessary for your preferred method of working in the rnd. Join for working in the rnd, being careful not to twist sts; pm for beginning of rnd. Purl 1 rnd.

BODY

Shape Body

Rnd 1: *K1-f/b; repeat from * to end—10 sts.

Rnd 2: *K1-f/b, k1; repeat from * to end—15 sts.

Rnd 3: *K1-f/b, p1, k1; repeat from * to end—20 sts.

Rnd 4: *K1-f/b, p2, k1; repeat from * to end—25 sts.

Rnd 5: *K1-f/b, k1, p2, k1; repeat from * to end—30 sts.

Rnd 6: *K1-f/b, k2, p2, k1; repeat from * to end—35 sts.

FINISHED MEASUREMENTS
24" radius, measured from center to tip of Point

YARN
Brown Sheep Company Burly Spun (100% wool; 130 yards / 8 ounces): 3 skeins #BS191 Kiwi

NEEDLES
One set of four, five, or six double-pointed needles (dpn) size US 13 (9 mm), and/or one or two 48" (120 cm) long or longer circular (circ) needle(s) size US 13 (9 mm)

One pair straight needles size US 13 (9 mm) (optional)

Change needle size if necessary to obtain correct gauge.

NOTIONS
Stitch markers; point protectors (optional)

GAUGE
13 sts and 14 rows = 4" (10 cm) in 2x2 Rib

start here ✖

Create a ribbed pentagon by increasing 5 times per round.

Rnd 7: *K1-f/b, p1, k2, p2, k1; repeat from * to end—40 sts.

Rnd 8: *K1-f/b, p2, k2, p2, k1; repeat from * to end—45 sts.

Rnd 9: *K1-f/b, k1, p2, k2, p2, k1; repeat from * to end—50 sts. Place markers every 10 sts (4 additional markers).

Rnd 10: [K1-f/b, *k2, p2; repeat from * to 1 st before marker, k1] 5 times—55 sts.

Rnd 11: [K1-f/b, p1, *k2, p2; repeat from * to 1 st before marker, k1] 5 times—60 sts.

Rnd 12: [K1-f/b, p2, *k2, p2; repeat from * to 1 st before marker, k1] 5 times—65 sts.

Rnd 13: [K1-f/b, k1, p2, *k2, p2; repeat from * to 1 st before marker, k1] 5 times—70 sts.

Repeat Rnds 10–13, increasing 5 sts each rnd, until piece measures 12" from center to needles (see Fig. 1).

POINTS

First Point

Note: You may wish to work each point on a second circ needle or a pair of straight needles, while leaving the remaining sts on the long circ needle. Use point protectors (optional) to secure held sts.

Row 1 (RS): Ssk, work in 2x2 Rib as established to marker, turn, removing marker—1 st decreased.

Row 2 (WS): Slip 1, work in 2x2 Rib as established to last 2 sts, p2tog-tbl, turn—1 st decreased.

Repeat Rows 1 and 2 until 1 st remains. *Note: If you have 2 sts left after the final repeat of Row 1, omit the slip 1 at the beginning of Row 2. Fasten off (see Fig. 2).*

Second Point

With RS facing, rejoin yarn to remaining sts. Work as for First Point. Repeat for remaining Points (see Fig. 3).

FINISHING

Block as desired.

VARIATIONS

You might like to try making this pattern larger or smaller than shown here or with yarn of a lighter—or even bulkier—gauge. Remember that yarn requirements will vary depending on what yarn you choose. If you substitute yarn or work to different dimensions, be sure to reserve half the yarn for forming the points of the Star to ensure that you don't run out.

FINDING FOUR

Four is the magic number for flat knitting. Increasing at a rate of approximately four stitches per round will almost always produce a flat shape. Here are examples of how I have used the Increase Rate of 4 in the blankets and shawls in this book.

In the Ripple Baby Blanket (page 123), there are 4 increases incorporated into every round.

In the Spiral Petal Shawl (page 106), the head of the Octopus (page 73), the heel of the Heel-up Socks (page 62), and the hand of the Half-Moon Mittens (page 49), there are 8 increases every other round.

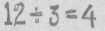
$$8 \div 2 = 4$$

At the top of the Hood-Down Hoodie (page 136), the hood increases by 12 stitches every 3 rounds.

$$12 \div 3 = 4$$

In the Queen Anne's Lace Blanket (page 88), each increase round contains 16 more increases than decreases. In the brim of the Sorting Hat (page 36), there are 16 increases every 4 rounds.

$$16 \div 4 = 4$$

In the Sunflower Shawl (page 96), there are 21 increases every 5 rounds.

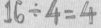
$$21 \div 5 = 4.2$$

Like every rule, this one has exceptions.

When the fabric is ribbed, the stitches are compacted horizontally, so a higher increase rate is needed to make the work lie flat. The Star Baby Blanket (shown here) contains 5 increases in each round. In the body of the Tree of Life Afghan (page 119), there are 40 new stitches created after every repeat of 8 rounds.

$$40 \div 8 = 5$$

In the Dahlia Blanket (page 92), a combination of increases and decreases makes the stitch pattern "biased," or diagonal. This also compacts the stitches horizontally, so the blanket still lies flat with a little bit of ruffling, even though there are 11 stitches increased every other row.

$$11 \div 2 = 5.5$$

tree of life afghan

This afghan was inspired by Yggdrasil, the World Tree in Norse mythology. Yggdrasil's branches extend far into the sky, and its roots extend deep underground. As this blanket grows, the smooth columns of knits envelop a growing number of purled clusters. New branches emerge from the right at four regular points, giving the afghan its gently sloping, rounded-square shape. An I-cord bind off gives the blanket a smooth scalloped edge.

SPECIAL ABBREVIATIONS

Inc4: [P1, k1, p1, k1, p1] into same st to increase from 1 st to 5 sts

Dec4: Sssk, slip st back to left-hand needle, k3tog to decrease from 5 sts to 1 st

STITCH PATTERN

Cocoon Stitch (for gauge swatch only)
Note: You may work Cocoon Stitch from text or Chart.
(multiple of 10 sts; 8-row repeat)
Row 1 (RS): *K2, dec4, k2, inc4; repeat from * to end.
Rows 2 and 4: *K5, p2, k1, p2; repeat from * to end.
Row 3: *K2, p1, k2, p5; repeat from * to end.
Row 5: *K2, inc4, k2, dec4; repeat from * to end.
Row 6: *K1, p2, k5, p2; repeat from * to end.
Row 7: *K2, p5, k2, p1; repeat from * to end.
Row 8: Repeat Row 6.
Repeat Rows 1–8 for Cocoon Stitch.

AFGHAN

Using Easy Circular CO (see page 144) or Disappearing Loop CO (see page 148), CO 8 sts. Divide sts among 2 or more needles if necessary for your preferred method of working in the rnd. Join for working in the rnd, being careful not to twist sts; pm (color A) for beginning of rnd.

Rnd 1: Knit.

Rnd 2: *K1, k1-f/b; repeat from * to end—12 sts.

Rnd 3: *RLI, k2, p1; repeat from * to end—16 sts.

FINISHED MEASUREMENTS
Approximately 48" wide

YARN
Brooklyn Tweed Shelter (100% Targhee-Columbia wool; 140 yards / 50 grams): 11 hanks #06 Tent

NEEDLES
One set of four or five double-pointed needles (dpn) size US 7 (4.5 mm), and/or one or two 40" (100 cm) long circular (circ) needle(s) size US 7 (4.5 mm)

One pair double-pointed needles size US 9 (5.5 mm)

Change needle size if necessary to obtain correct gauge.

NOTIONS
Stitch markers (1 in color A for beginning of rnd; 3 in color B); waste yarn

GAUGE
22 sts and 28 rows = 4" (10 cm) in Cocoon Stitch, using smaller needles

Rnd 4: *K3, LLI, p1; repeat from * to end—20 sts.

Rnd 5: *K4, inc4; repeat from * to end—36 sts.

Rnd 6: *K2, LLI, k2, p5; repeat from * to end—40 sts.

Rnd 7: *RLI, k2, p1, k2, p5; repeat from * to end—44 sts.

Rnd 8: *K3, LLI, p1, k2, p5; repeat from * to end—48 sts.

Rnd 9: *K4, inc4, k2, dec4; repeat from * to end.

Rnd 10: *K2, LLI, k2, p5, k2, p1; repeat from * to end—52 sts.

Rnd 11: *RLI, k2, p1, k2, p5, k2, p1; repeat from * to end—56 sts.

Rnd 12: *K3, LLI, p1, k2, p5, k2, p1; repeat from * to end—60 sts.

Rnd 13: *K4, inc4, k2, dec4, k2, inc4; repeat from * to end of round—76 sts. Place 3 additional markers (color B) every 19 sts.

BODY

Note: Change to circ needle(s) if necessary for number of sts on needle(s). You may work Body from text or Body Chart.

Rnd 1: [K2, LLI, k2, p5, *k2, p1, k2, p5; repeat from * to marker] 4 times—80 sts (1 st increased between markers).

Rnd 2: [RLI, k2, p1, k2, p5, *k2, p1, k2, p5; repeat from * to marker] 4 times—84 sts (1 st increased between markers).

Rnd 3: [K3, LLI, p1, k2, p5, *k2, p1, k2, p5; repeat from * to marker] 4 times—88 sts (1 st increased between markers).

Rnd 4: [K4, inc4, k2, dec4, *k2, inc4, k2, dec4; repeat from * to marker] 4 times.

Rnd 5: [K2, LLI, *k2, p5, k2, p1; repeat from * to marker] 4 times—92 sts (1 st increased between markers).

Rnd 6: [RLI, k2, p1, *k2, p5, k2, p1; repeat from * to marker] 4 times—96 sts (1 st increased between markers).

Rnd 7: [K3, LLI, p1, *k2, p5, k2, p1; repeat from * to marker] 4 times—100 sts (1 st increased between markers).

Rnd 8: [K4, inc4, *k2, dec4, k2, inc4; repeat from * to marker] 4 times—116 sts (4 sts increased between markers).

COCOON STITCH*

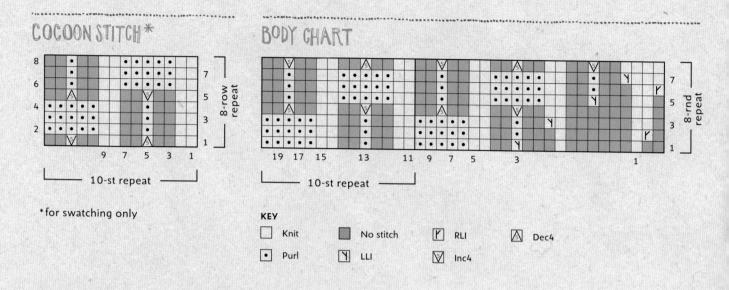

*for swatching only

BODY CHART

KEY

☐ Knit	▦ No stitch	⅄ RLI	⅄ Dec4
• Purl	⅄ LLI	⅄ Inc4	

Repeat Rnds 1–8 until piece measures 20" from center to edge, measuring to center of any section. *Note: You may wish to transfer one section of sts to waste yarn or a second circ needle to ensure accurate measurement. Do not break yarn.*

I-cord BO

Using waste yarn and larger dpns, CO 3 sts. With yarn attached to Body, and working I-cord (see page 10), *k2, ssk (last st on dpn together with 1 st from Body; repeat from * until all sts from Body have been worked. Carefully unravel waste yarn and place live sts on second dpn. Using Kitchener st (see page 154), graft live sts.

FINISHING

Block as desired.

VARIATIONS

This pattern will work as written with yarns of many gauges. If you wish to make a blanket of different dimensions, simply repeat Body Rounds 1–8 to desired measurements before beginning the I-cord bind-off. Remember that variations will also affect yarn requirements.

ripple baby blanket

The purl stitches that swirl outward from the blanket center remind me of the ripples made by raindrops on the surface of a pond. To make the spiral, you divide the work into seven sections, then work a pattern of knits, purls, and increases eight times. Since each repeat ends one section to the left of where it began, the pattern spirals around and around as the blanket grows. You finish with a picot bind-off, giving the edge a fringe for little fingers to grab.

FINISHED MEASUREMENTS

36" diameter

YARN

Madelinetosh Tosh Vintage (100% superwash merino wool; 200 yards / 100 grams): 5 hanks Fathom

NEEDLES

One set of four or five double-pointed needles (dpn) size US 6 (4 mm), and/or one or two 60" (150 cm) circular (circ) needle(s) size US 6 (4 mm)

Change needle size if necessary to obtain correct gauge.

NOTIONS

Stitch markers

GAUGE

20 sts and 26 rows = 4" (10 cm) in Stockinette stitch (St st)

BLANKET

Using Easy Circular CO (see page 144) or Disappearing Loop CO (see page 148), CO 7 sts. Divide sts among 2 or more needles if necessary for your preferred method of working in the rnd. Join for working in the rnd, being careful not to twist sts; do not place a marker for beginning of rnd. Knit 1 rnd.

Set Up Spiral

Rnd 1: [Yo, k1] 7 times—14 sts.

Rnd 2: Knit.

Rnds 3–6: P6, knit to first purl st, [yo, k1] twice—22 sts after Rnd 6.

Rnd 7: P8, knit to first purl st, [yo, k1] twice—24 sts.

Rnd 8: P10, knit to first purl st, [yo, k1] twice—26 sts.

Rnd 9: P12, knit to first purl st, [yo, k1] twice—28 sts.

Place markers every 4 sts to mark 7 sections.

Body

Note: Change to circ needle(s) if necessary for number of sts on needle(s). Since each rnd is worked over 8 sections, you will work last (increase) section over first section that you worked at beginning of that rnd; this will shift each rnd 1 section to left. Increase Section will always begin above first purl st from rnd below.

Body Increase Rnd: Purl all sts for 3 sections, knit all sts for 4 sections, work Increase Section as indicated in Body Increase Table (see page 124). Work each Body Increase Rnd a total of 7 times, until you have the same number of sts in each section; then move on to the following Body Increase Rnd. Continue in this

BODY INCREASE TABLE

BODY INCREASE ROUND NUMBER	STITCH COUNT IN INCREASE SECTION BEFORE WORKING INCREASES	INSTRUCTIONS FOR INCREASE SECTION*	FINAL STITCH COUNT IN INCREASE SECTION AFTER WORKING INCREASES
1	4	[Yo, k1] 4 times	8
2	8	[Yo, k1, yo, k2tog, yo, k1] twice	12
3	12	[Yo, k1, yo, k2tog] 4 times	16
4	16	[Yo, k1, (yo, k2tog) twice, yo, k1, yo, k2tog] twice	20
5	20	[Yo, k1, (yo, k2tog) twice] 4 times	24
6	24	[Yo, k1, (yo, k2tog) 3 times, yo, k1, (yo, k2tog) twice] twice	28
7	28	[Yo, k1, (yo, k2tog) 3 times] 4 times	32
8	32	[Yo, k1, (yo, k2tog) 4 times, yo, k1, (yo, k2tog) 3 times] twice	36
9	36	[Yo, k1, (yo, k2tog) 4 times] 4 times	40
10	40	[Yo, k1, (yo, k2tog) 5 times, yo, k1, (yo, k2tog) 4 times] twice	44
11	44	[Yo, k1, (yo, k2tog) 5 times] 4 times	48
12	48	[Yo, k1, (yo, k2tog) 6 times, yo, k1, (yo, k2tog) 5 times] twice	52
13	52	[Yo, k1, (yo, k2tog) 6 times] 4 times	56
14	56	[Yo, k1, (yo, k2tog) 7 times, yo, k1, (yo, k2tog) 6 times] twice	60
15	60	[Yo, k1, (yo, k2tog) 7 times] 4 times	64
16	64	[Yo, k1, (yo, k2tog) 8 times, yo, k1, (yo, k2tog) 7 times] twice	68
17	68	[Yo, k1, (yo, k2tog) 8 times] 4 times	72
18	72	[Yo, k1, (yo, k2tog) 9 times, yo, k1, (yo, k2tog) 8 times] twice. *Note: Piece should measure approximately 18" from center to outside edge at this point. Work additional Body Increase Rnds if needed or desired.*	76
19	76	[Yo, k1, (yo, k2tog) 9 times] 4 times	80
20	80	[Yo, k1, (yo, k2tog) 10 times, yo, k1, (yo, k2tog) 9 times] twice	84
21	84	[Yo, k1, (yo, k2tog) 10 times] 4 times	88
22	88	[Yo, k1, (yo, k2tog) 11 times, yo, k1, (yo, k2tog) 10 times] twice	92
23	92	[Yo, k1, (yo, k2tog) 11 times] 4 times	96
24	96	[Yo, k1, (yo, k2tog) 12 times, yo, k1, (yo, k2tog) 11 times] twice	100

*This chart includes instructions for more Body Increase Rnds than required for blanket shown in case you want to continue.

manner until you have completed Body Increase Rnd 18, and have 76 sts in each section (you will have 18 purl ridges; piece should measure approximately 18" from center to outside edge).

Note: To find your place in the Body Increase Table, when you are about to work an Increase Section, count the number of sts in the next section on the needle, then find your st count in the second column of the table.

Final Spiral

Note: Change to working back and forth. You will be working 1 less section on each row.

Row 1 (RS): Purl all sts for 3 sections, knit all sts for 4 sections, turn.

Row 2 (WS): Purl for 3 sections, knit for 3 sections, turn. Break yarn.

Row 3: Slip 1 section without working it. Rejoin yarn, purl for 3 sections, knit for 2 sections, turn.

Row 4: Purl for 1 section, knit for 3 sections, turn. Break yarn.

Row 5: Slip 1 section without working it. Rejoin yarn, purl for 3 sections, turn.

Row 6: Knit for 2 sections, turn. Break yarn.

Row 7: Slip 1 section without working it. Rejoin yarn, purl to end, turn.

Picot BO Row: Using Knitted CO (see page 155), *CO 3 sts, BO 5 sts; repeat from * until all sts have been BO.

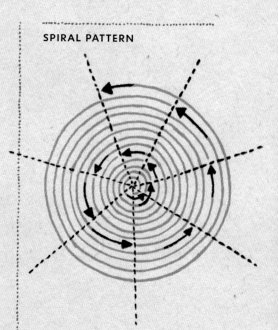

SPIRAL PATTERN

Each repeat ends 1 section to the left of where it began.

SPIRALS MADE OF SPIRALS MADE OF SPIRALS

This blanket pattern is my attempt to create a knitted version of an Archimedian spiral, named for the ancient Greek mathematician Archimedes. In an Archimedian spiral, each turning of the spiral arm has a constant separation distance, meaning that each successive turn of the spiral will appear to be parallel to the last, like the grooves in a record album or CD.

In this blanket, each of the raised purl ridges of the spiral is separated by four rounds of knits and increases, so each section of purl ridges appears to be parallel to the one before it. But if you think about it, revolutionary knitting is already a kind of spiral, since each round of knitting continues moving to the left, one round above the last. Even when working I-cord, the tube of knitting forms a helix, or vertical twist, as though each stitch is taking one step up a spiral staircase. So by knitting a spiral motif in this blanket, I'm using one spiral to "draw" another.

The yarn I used for this project is made of four small strands, or plies, of yarn. Each of those plies is itself a helix or spiral staircase of twisted wool, and those helices are wrapped around one another to make the yarn—so when I made this project I was drawing a spiral by knitting a spiral with a yarn that's made of spirals.

SWEATERS

Sometimes the biggest challenge of designing garments from the center out can be deciding where to start. Since the ability to work outward from just about any point we choose offers so many options, "Where should I begin?" can feel like an open-ended question. The three sweaters in this chapter explore just a few of the possible starting places that presented themselves to me. One starts at the top of a hood, which morphs to become part of the shoulder shaping. Another is worked downward from the collar. And the third adapts center-out knitting to working inward from the sleeves.

geometric shrug

My inspiration for the shaping of this sweater came from an unlikely source: mittens. If you've worked the Half-Moon Mittens on page 49, the construction of this shrug will feel familiar. In the same way that those mittens expand from the base of the thumb to cover the hand, you work the sleeves of this shrug upward from the cuff, then expand each sleeve until an octagon emerges around it to become the body. At this point, I have to admit the work starts looking like the heads of two elephants, with sleeves for trunks. With faith, you then join the two symmetrical sleeve pieces with a short seam down the back. Then you transfer the live stitches from each piece to a single needle and work a ribbed edging all around. The result, rather than an elephant, is a snug-fitting shrug that, the women in my life tell me, is a very useful and versatile wardrobe addition.

SIZES

X-Small/Small (Medium/Large, X-Large/2X-Large)

FINISHED MEASUREMENTS

35 (43, 51)" chest, overlapped

YARN

Malabrigo Merino Worsted (100% merino wool; 210 yards / 100 grams): 4 (4, 5) hanks #99 Stone Blue

NEEDLES

One set of five double-pointed needles (dpn) size US 10 (6 mm)

Two or three 36" (90 cm) long or longer circular (circ) needles, size US 10 (6 mm)

One 48" (120 cm) long or longer circular needle size US 10 (6 mm)

Change needle size if necessary to obtain correct gauge.

NOTIONS

Stitch markers

GAUGE

16 sts and 23 rows = 4" in Stockinette Stitch (St st)

STITCH PATTERN

1x1 Rib (multiple of 2 sts; 1-rnd repeat)
All Rnds: *K1, p1; repeat from * to end.

RIGHT SLEEVE

Using dpns, CO 28 (32, 36) sts. Join for working in the rnd, being careful not to twist sts; pm for beginning of rnd. Begin 1x1 Rib; work even for 2".

Shape Sleeve

Next Rnd: Change to St st. Increase 2 sts this rnd, then every 8 (6, 5) rnds 9 (12, 15) times, as follows: K1, M1, knit to last st, M1, k1—48 (58, 68) sts. Work even until piece measures 18" from the beginning.

RIGHT FRONT/BACK

Next Rnd: K4 (8, 12), pm, [k1, pm] 4 times, k32 (34, 36), [pm, k1] 4 times, pm, k4 (8, 12).

Shape Right Front/Back

Next Rnd: Increase 8 sts this rnd, then every other rnd 14 times, as follows: Knit to first marker, [knit to 1 st before next marker, RLI, k1] 4 times, knit to marker, [k1, LLI, knit to marker] 4 times, knit to end—168 (178, 188) sts [4 (8, 12)-16-16-16-16-32 (34, 36)-16-16-16-16-4 (8, 12) sts]. Knit 1 rnd.

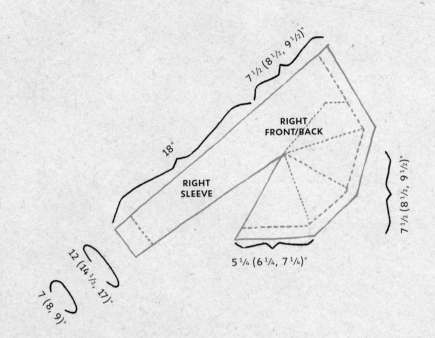

RIGHT FRONT/BACK

RIGHT SLEEVE

7 ½ (8 ½, 9 ½)"

18"

12 (14 ½, 17)"

7 (8, 9)"

5 ¼ (6 ¼, 7 ¼)"

7 ½ (8 ½, 9 ½)"

Shape Shoulder

Rnd 1: Knit to first marker, [knit to 1 st before marker, RLI, k1] 3 times, knit to 2 sts before marker, k2tog, knit to marker, ssk, knit to marker, [k1, LLI, knit to marker] 3 times, knit to end—172 (182, 192) sts [4 (8, 12)-17-17-17-15-32 (34, 36)-15-17-17-17-4 (8, 12) sts].

Rnd 2: Knit.

Rnd 3: Knit to first marker, [knit to 1 st before marker, RLI, k1] 3 times, knit to 2 sts before marker, k2tog, knit to seventh marker, [k1, LLI, knit to marker] 3 times, knit to end.

Rnd 4: Knit.

Repeat Rnds 1–4 two (3, 5) times, then Rnds 1 and 2 zero (1, 0) time(s)—195 (218, 242) sts [4 (8, 12)-22 (25, 28)-22 (25, 28)-22 (25, 28)-10 (7, 4)-32 (34, 36)-13 (11, 10)-22 (25, 28)-22 (25, 28)-22 (25, 28)-4 (8, 12) sts]. Break yarn. Slip first 6 sections to right-hand needle; the first section on the left-hand needle should have 13 (11, 10) sts in it; leave sts on one circ needle and set aside.

LEFT SLEEVE

Work as for Right Sleeve to beginning of shoulder shaping—168 (178, 188) sts [4 (8, 12)-16-16-16-16-32 (34, 36)-16-16-16-16-4 (8, 12) sts].

Shape Shoulder

Rnd 1: Knit to first marker, [knit to 1 st before marker, RLI, k1] 3 times, knit to 2 sts before marker, k2tog, knit to marker, ssk, knit to marker, [k1, LLI, knit to marker] 3 times, knit to end—172 (182, 192) sts [4 (8, 12)-17-17-17-15-32 (34, 36)-15-17-17-17-4 (8, 12) sts].

Rnd 2: Knit.

Rnd 3: Knit to first marker, [knit to 1 st before marker, RLI, k1] 3 times, knit to sixth marker, ssk, knit to marker, [k1, LLI, knit to marker] 3 times, knit to end.

Rnd 4: Knit.

Repeat Rnds 1–4 two (3, 5) times, then Rnds 1 and 2 zero (1, 0) time(s)—195 (218, 242) sts [4 (8, 12)-22 (25, 28)-22 (25, 28)-22 (25, 28)-13 (10, 11)-32 (34, 36)-10 (7, 4)- 22 (25, 28)-22 (25, 28)-22 (25, 28)-4 (8, 12) sts]. Do not break yarn; slip first 5 sections to right-hand needle; the first section on the left-hand needle should have 32 (34, 36) sts in it.

FINISHING

Using Kitchener st (see page 154) and separate strand of yarn, and with sts from Left Front/Back held in front, join next 35 (35, 39) sts from each piece (2 full sections) for Back seam.

Neck and Body Band: Slip Left Front/Back sts back to left-hand needle until you are back to the beginning of the rnd, where the working yarn is. Using longer circ needle, knit around Left Front/Back to Back seam, knit around Right Front/Back to next Back seam, knit around Left-Front/Back to end, removing all markers; pm for beginning of rnd—320 (364, 408) sts. Change to 1x1 Rib; work even for 1". BO all sts in pattern.

Block as desired.

leaf-yoke sweater

This sweater combines a few ideas that usually don't go together: lace knit with fuzzy, slubby yarn, and inspiration from two of my knitting heroes, whose design sensibilities were quite different—Elizabeth Zimmermann and Marianne Kinzel.

Elizabeth Zimmermann encouraged creativity in every knitter, often giving general guidelines and ideas rather than round-by-round patterns. Kinzel, on the other hand, was an absolute master of center-out lace projects. For me, looking at Kinzel's work is like listening to Bach, with her beautiful and precise floral symmetries coming together just so. Her written patterns are painstakingly spelled out stitch by stitch and row by row. Taking the basic architecture of a yoked sweater that Zimmermann describes in her book *Knitting Workshop* as my starting point, I worked this sweater from the top down with a Kinzel-inspired leaf pattern.

STITCH PATTERNS

3x2 Rib (multiple of 5 sts; 1-rnd repeat)
All Rnds: *K3, p2; repeat from * to end.

Left Leaf (multiple of 10 sts; 8 rnds) (see Chart)
Rnd 1: *Yo, k1, yo, sssk, k6; repeat from * to end.
Rnds 2, 4, and 6: Knit.
Rnd 3: *[K1, yo] twice, k1, sssk, k4; repeat from * to end.
Rnd 5: *K2, yo, k1, yo, k2, sssk, k2; repeat from * to end.
Rnd 7: *K3, yo, k1, yo, k3, sssk; repeat from * to end.
Rnd 8: Knit.

Right Leaf (multiple of 10 sts; 8 rnds) (see Chart)
Rnd 1: *K6, k3tog, yo, k1, yo; repeat from * to end.
Rnds 2, 4, and 6: Knit.
Rnd 3: *K4, k3tog, [k1, yo] twice, k1; repeat from * to end.
Rnd 5: *K2, k3tog, k2, yo, k1, yo, k2; repeat from * to end.
Rnd 7: *K3tog, k3, yo, k1, yo, k3; repeat from * to end.
Rnd 8: Knit.

SIZES

X-Small (Small, Medium, Large, X-Large, 2X-Large, 3X-Large, 4X-Large, 5X-Large)

FINISHED MEASUREMENTS

32 1/2 (36 1/2, 40, 44, 47 1/2, 51 1/2, 55 1/4, 58 1/2, 62 1/2)" bust

YARN

The Fibre Company Acadia (60% merino wool / 20% baby alpaca / 20% silk; 149 yards / 50 grams) 6 (6, 7, 8, 8, 9, 10, 11, 12) hanks Wild Onion

NEEDLES

One 16" (40 cm) long circular (circ) needle size US 6 (4.5 mm)

One 29" (70 cm) long or longer circular needle size US 6 (4.5 mm)

One set of five double-pointed needles (dpn) size US 6 (4.5 mm)

Change needle size if necessary to obtain correct gauge.

NOTIONS

Stitch markers; waste yarn

GAUGE

20 sts and 32 rnds = 4" (10 cm) in Reverse Stockinette stitch (Rev St st)

24 sts and 38 rnds = 4" (10 cm) in Leaf Pattern

Leaf Points (multiple of 10 sts; 5 rnds)
(see Chart)

Rnd 1: *K7, k2tog, yo, k1; repeat from * to end.

Rnd 2: *Ssk, k5, k2tog, M1-p, p1, M1-p; repeat from * to end.

Rnd 3: *M1-p, ssk, k3, k2tog, M1-p, p3; repeat from * to end.

Rnd 4: *P1, M1-p, ssk, k1, k2tog, M1-p, p4; repeat from * to end.

Rnd 5: *P2, M1-p, s2kp2, M1-p, p5; repeat from * to end.

Note: For some sizes, you omit some or all of the M1-ps on Rnd 5. There are 2 M1-ps per repeat; the instructions will tell you in how many repeats you omit both M1-ps. When working omissions, spread them out as evenly as possible (e.g., if you have 30 pattern repeats, and you are to omit M1-ps from 10 of those repeats, alternate 2 repeats including M1-ps with 1 repeat omitting them.)

1x4 Rib (multiple of 5 sts; 1-rnd repeat)
All Rnds: *K1, p4; repeat from * to end.

Alternating Rib
(multiple of 5 sts; 1-rnd repeat)
All Rnds: *K1, p1, k2, p1; repeat from * to end.

1x1 Rib (multiple of 2 sts; 1-rnd repeat)
All Rnds: *K1, p1; repeat from * to end.

INCREASE RNDS
FOR YOKE SHAPING

Increase Rnd A: *K10, [k1, CO 1] 10 times; repeat from * to end.

Increase Rnd B: *K10, [k1, CO 1] 10 times; repeat from * to last 10 sts, k10.

Increase Rnd C: *K10, [CO 1, k1] 10 times; repeat from * to end.

Increase Rnd D: [CO1, k1] 10 times, knit to last 10 sts, [CO 1, k1] 10 times.

Increase Rnd E: [K1, CO 1] 10 times, knit to last 10 sts, [k1, CO 1] 10 times.

Increase Rnd F: *[CO 1, k1] 10 times, k10; repeat from * to end.

Increase Rnd G: *[CO 1, k1] 10 times, k10; repeat from * to last 10 sts, [CO 1, k1] 10 times.

Increase Rnd H: *[K1, CO 1] 10 times, k10; repeat from * to last 10 sts, [k1, CO 1] 10 times.

Increase Rnd I: K10, *[k1, CO 1] 10 times, k10; repeat from * to end.

Increase Rnd J: K20, *[k1, CO 1] 10 times, k10; repeat from * to end.

Increase Rnd K: *K10, [CO 1, k1] 10 times; repeat from * to last 10 sts, k10.

Increase Rnd L: *[K1, CO 1] 10 times, k10; repeat from * to end.

YOKE

Note: After first CO, use Backward Loop CO (see page 154) for any other COs.

Using shorter circ needle or dpns, CO 80 (90, 90, 100, 100, 110, 110, 120, 120) sts. Begin 3x2 Rib; work even for 1". Change to Right (Right, Right, Left, Left, Left, Left, Right, Right) Leaf; work even for 8 rnds.

Shape Yoke

Increase Rnd: Work Increase Rnd A (B, B, C, C, D, D, E, E)—120 (130, 130, 150, 150, 130, 130, 140, 140) sts. Work Left (Left, Left, Right, Right, Right, Right, Left, Left) Leaf Pattern for 8 rnds.

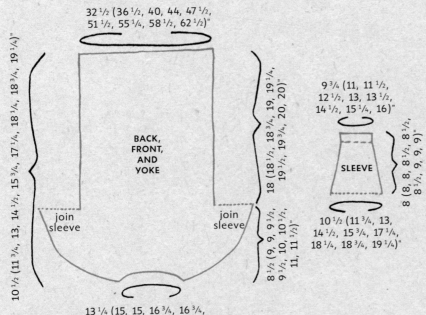

32 ½ (36 ½, 40, 44, 47 ½, 51 ½, 55 ¼, 58 ½, 62 ½)"

10 ½ (11 ¾, 13, 14 ½, 15 ¾, 17 ¼, 18 ¼, 18 ¾, 19 ¼)"

BACK, FRONT, AND YOKE

18 (18 ½, 18 ¾, 19, 19 ½, 19 ¾, 19 ½, 20, 20)"

join sleeve

join sleeve

8 ½ (9, 9, 9 ½, 9 ½, 10, 10 ½, 11, 11 ½)"

13 ¼ (15, 15, 16 ¾, 16 ¾, 18 ¼, 18 ¼, 20, 20)"

9 ¾ (11, 11 ½, 12 ½, 13, 13 ½, 14 ½, 15 ¼, 16)"

SLEEVE

8 (8, 8 ½, 8 ½, 8 ½, 9, 9, 9)"

10 ½ (11 ¾, 13, 14 ½, 15 ¾, 17 ¼, 18 ¼, 18 ¾, 19 ¼)"

Increase Rnd: Work Increase Rnd F (G, G, H, H, I, I, F, F)—180 (200, 200, 230, 230, 190, 190, 210, 210) sts. Work Right (Right, Right, Left, Left, Left, Left, Right, Right) Leaf Pattern for 8 rnds.

Increase Rnd: Work Increase Rnd A (J, J, G, G, K, K, I, I)—270 (290, 290, 350, 350, 280, 280, 310, 310) sts. Work Left (Left, Left, Right, Right, Right, Right, Left, Left) Leaf Pattern for 8 rnds.

SIZES 2X-LARGE, 3X-LARGE, 4X-LARGE, AND 5X-LARGE ONLY

Increase Rnd: Work Increase Rnd - (-, -, -, -, L, L, G, G)— - (-, -, -, -, 420, 420, 470, 470) sts. Work - (-, -, -, -, Left, Left, Right, Right) Leaf Pattern for 8 rnds.

SIZES LARGE, X-LARGE, 4X-LARGE, AND 5X-LARGE ONLY

Work Left Leaf Pattern for 8 rnds.

ALL SIZES

Next Rnd: Change to Leaf Points; work even for 5 rnds, omitting both

M1-ps in 27 (25, 12, 29, 15, 37, 25, 43, 35) repeats of Rnd 5 (see Note on page 134)—216 (240, 266, 292, 320, 346, 370, 384, 400) sts remain.

Next Rnd: Change to Reverse St st; work even until piece measures 8 ½ (9, 9, 9 ½, 9 ½, 10, 10 ½, 11, 11 ½)" from the beginning.

BODY

Join Back and Front: P34 (38, 42, 46, 50, 54, 58, 61, 65) sts for right side of Back, transfer next 40 (44, 49, 54, 60, 65, 69, 70, 70) sts to waste yarn for Right Sleeve, CO 26 (30, 32, 36, 38, 42, 44, 48, 52) sts for underarm, p68 (76, 84, 92, 100, 108, 116, 122, 130) sts for Front, transfer next 40 (44, 49, 54, 60, 65, 69, 70, 70) sts to waste yarn for Left Sleeve, CO 26 (30, 32, 36, 38, 42, 44, 48, 52) sts for underarm, purl to end for Left Back.

Next Rnd: *Purl to CO sts, [p1, slip next st to waste yarn for Sleeve underarm] 13 (15, 16, 18, 19, 21, 22, 24, 26) times; repeat from * once, purl to end—162

(182, 200, 220, 238, 258, 276, 292, 312) sts. Work even until piece measures 14 ½ (15, 15 ¼, 15 ½, 15 ¾, 16, 16 ¼, 16 ½, 16 ½)" from underarm, increase 0 (0, 0, 0, 2, 2, 0, 0, 0) sts or decrease 2 (2, 0, 0, 0, 0, 1, 2, 2) sts evenly on last rnd—160 (180, 200, 220, 240, 260, 275, 290, 310) sts.

Next Rnd: Change to 1x4 Rib; work even for 2 ½". Change to Alternating Rib; work even for 1". BO all sts in pattern.

SLEEVES

Transfer Sleeve sts to dpns or shorter circ needle, including underarm sts. With RS facing, rejoin yarn at center of underarm—53 (59, 65, 72, 79, 86, 91, 94, 96) sts. Join for working in the rnd; pm for beginning of rnd. Begin Rev St st; work even for 1 rnd.

Shape Sleeve

Next Rnd: Decrease 2 sts this rnd, then every 20 (20, 10, 9, 6, 5, 5, 5, 6) rnds 1 (1, 3, 4, 6, 8, 8, 8, 7) time(s), as follows: P1, p2tog, purl to last 3 sts, p2tog, p1—49 (55, 57, 62, 65, 68, 73, 76, 80) sts remain. Work even until piece measures 7 (7, 7, 7 ½, 7 ½, 7 ½, 8, 8, 8)" from underarm, decrease 1 (1, 1, 0, 1, 0, 1, 0, 0) st(s) on last rnd—48 (54, 56, 62, 64, 68, 72, 76, 80) sts remain.

Next Rnd: Change to 1x1 Rib; work even for 1". BO all sts in pattern.

To finish, block as desired.

LEAF PATTERNS

LEFT LEAF

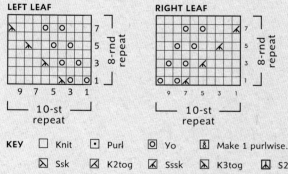

9 7 5 3 1

10-st repeat

8-rnd repeat

RIGHT LEAF

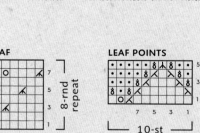

9 7 5 3 1

10-st repeat

8-rnd repeat

LEAF POINTS

7 5 3 1

10-st repeat

5-rnd repeat

KEY

☐ Knit   • Purl   Ⓞ Yo   ⑧ Make 1 purlwise.

⊠ Ssk   ⋌ K2tog   ⋋ Sssk   ⋉ K3tog   ⋏ S2kp2

135

hood-down hoodie

This sweater begins at the center of the hood. To start, you work a hexagon shape, increasing at six regular points. Then you separate each of the six sides of the hexagon with two purl stitches, creating a slight ribbing in the fabric. After the hood grows wide enough to cover the head, you continue back and forth until it reaches the shoulders. At the shoulders, you resume increasing, expanding the hexagonal shape again. Then, in a moment of knitter's origami, you fold the hexagon to reveal the sweater shape—two of the six sections become sleeves, while the four remaining sections become the front and back.

To keep things interesting while working down the trunk, I used double-knitting to make the half-kangaroo pockets. Instead of working each pocket separately and sewing it into place like a patch, both sides of each pocket are worked as you complete each row.

STITCH PATTERN

1x1 Rib (multiple of 2 sts; 1-row/rnd repeat)
Row/Rnd 1: *K1, p1; repeat from * to end, end k1 if an odd number of sts.
Row/Rnd 2: Knit the knit sts and purl the purl sts as they face you.
Repeat Row/Rnd 2 for 1x1 Rib.

SPECIAL TECHNIQUE

Double-Knitting: The Pockets are worked using Double-Knitting. In Double-Knitting, you are creating 2 separate fabrics at the same time by working every other stitch and slipping the alternate stitches on one pass of the row; on the following pass, you will work the stitches you slipped and slip the stitches you worked on the previous row. For this pattern, each Pocket row consists of 1 full pass across all of the stitches, and 2 half passes worked on just one Pocket.

On the first Setup Row (1), you will double the number of Pocket stitches so that you can use half of the stitches for the inside of the Pocket and half for the outside. On the Second Setup Row, you will slip the outside Pocket stitches and purl the inside Pocket stitches for both Pockets on the first pass (2a), knit the outside stitches and slip the inside stitches of the left Pocket only on the second pass (2b), then work the left Pocket and selvage stitches on the third pass (2c).

SIZES

Small (Medium, Large, X-Large, 2X-Large, 3X-Large)

FINISHED MEASUREMENTS

34 ¾ (38 ¾, 42 ¾, 46 ¾, 50 ¾, 54 ¾)" chest

YARN

Swans Island Natural Blends Worsted Weight (85% organic merino wool / 15% alpaca; 250 yards / 100 grams): 6 (7, 7, 8, 8, 9) hanks Sea Smoke

NEEDLES

One set of four or five double-pointed needles (dpn) size US 6 (4 mm), or one 36" (90 cm) long or longer circular (circ) needle

One set of four or five double-pointed needles size US 4 (3.5 mm), or one 36" (90 cm) long or longer circular needle

Change needle size if necessary to obtain correct gauge.

NOTIONS

Stitch markers; waste yarn; safety pins; 19 (20, 20, 21, 21, 22)" separating zipper; sewing needle and matching thread

GAUGE

20 sts and 28 rows = 4" (10 cm) in Stockinette st (St st), using larger needles

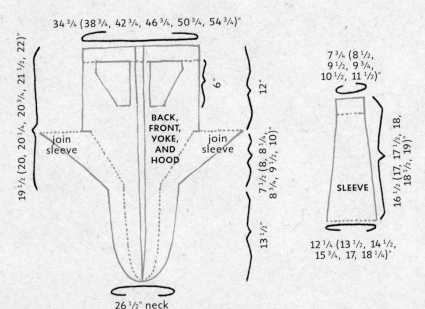

34 ¾ (38 ¾, 42 ¾, 46 ¾, 50 ¾, 54 ¾)"

19 ½ (20, 20 ¼, 20 ¾, 21 ½, 22)"

6"

12"

BACK,
FRONT,
YOKE,
AND
HOOD

join sleeve

join sleeve

7 ½ (8, 8 ¼, 8 ¾, 9 ½, 10)"

13 ½"

26 ½" neck

7 ¾ (8 ½, 9 ½, 9 ¾, 10 ½, 11 ½)"

SLEEVE

16 ½ (17, 17 ½, 18, 18 ½, 19)"

12 ¼ (13 ½, 14 ½, 15 ¾, 17, 18 ¼)"

On the Third Setup Row, you will knit the outside stitches and slip the inside stitches of both Pockets on the first pass (3a), purl the inside stitches and slip the outside stitches of the right Pocket only on the second pass (3b), then work the right Pocket and selvage stitches on the third pass (3c). Once these Setup Rows are complete, you will continue to work in the same manner, while shaping the opening edge of the Pockets.

Once you are finished with the shaping of the open edge of the Pockets, you will join the open edge of the Pockets to the fabric of the Body. On the first pass (a wrong-side row), you will purl the outside stitches and slip the inside stitches of the right Pocket and slip the outside stitches

and purl the inside stitches of the left Pocket on the first pass (1a), slip the inside stitches and knit the outside stitches of the left Pocket only on the second pass (1b), then slip the outside stitches and purl the inside stitches of the left Pocket on the third pass (1c). On Row 2, you will work as established across the left Pocket, knit the outside stitches and slip the inside stitches of the right Pocket on the first pass (2a), purl the inside stitches and slip the outside stitches of the right Pocket only on the second pass (2b), then knit the outside stitches and slip the inside stitches of the right Pocket on the third pass (2b). You will continue to work in the same manner until you are ready to rejoin the Pockets by working the inside and outside pocket stitches together.

Always be sure to slip the stitches with the yarn in the correct position, as instructed; otherwise, your separate fabrics will end up being joined.

HOOD

Using larger needles and Easy Circular CO (see page 144) or Disappearing Loop CO (see page 148), CO 18 sts.

Rnd 1: P1, *k1, p2; repeat from * to last 2 sts, k1, p1.

Shape Top of Hood
Rnd 2: P1, *[k1, yo, k1] into same st, p1, pm, p1; repeat from * to last 2 sts, [k1, yo, k1] into same st, p1—30 sts.

Rnds 3–4: Knit the knit sts and purl the purl sts as they face you; knit all yos.

Rnd 5: P1, [RLI, knit to 1 st before marker, LLI, p1, sm, p1] 5 times, RLI, knit to last st, LLI, p1—42 sts.

Repeat Rnds 3–5 seven times—126 sts (21 sts between markers) (see Fig. 1).

Shape Sides of Hood

Note: Change to working back and forth. Remove third (center) marker.

Row 1 (RS): Using Knitted CO (see page 155), CO 6 sts, k5, p2, work to end, remove beginning-of-rnd marker, pick up and knit 6 sts from the WS of the CO sts, p1, k5—138 sts.

Row 2: Slip 5, k2, work to end.

Row 3: Slip 5, p2, work to end. Work even until piece measures 13 ½" from the beginning, ending with a WS row (see Fig. 2).

Next Row (RS): K1, BO next 3 sts, work to end—135 sts remain.

Next Row: P1, BO next 3 sts, work to end—132 sts remain.

Shape Back Neck

Note: Back neck is shaped using short rows (see page 156); work wraps together with wrapped sts as you come to them.

Row 1 (RS): Slip 2, p2, work 75 sts, wrp-t.

Row 2: Work 26 sts, wrp-t.

Row 3: Work 30 sts, wrp-t.

Row 4: Work 34 sts, wrp-t.

Row 5: Work 37 sts, work to end.

Row 6: Slip 2, k2, work across all sts.

Rows 7–12: Repeat Rows 1–6.

YOKE

Increase Row 1: Continuing to work in pattern as established, increase 8 sts this row, every other row 7 (13, 20, 22, 24, 26) times, then every 4 rows 9 (5, 0, 0, 0, 0) times, as follows: [Work to 1 st before marker, M1-l, p1, sm, p1, M1-r] 4 times, work to end—268 (284, 300, 316, 332, 348) sts. Work even for 3 (3, 1, 1, 1, 1) row(s).

SIZES MEDIUM TO 2X-LARGE ONLY

Increase Row 2: Increase 4 sts this row, every other row – (0, 0, 3, 7, 7) times, then every 4 rows – (1, 3, 2, 0, 0) time(s), as follows: Work to 1 st before first marker, M1-l, p1, sm, work to second marker, sm, p1, M1-r, work to 1 st before third marker, M1-l, p1, sm, work to fourth marker, sm, p1, M1-r, work to end— – (292, 316, 340, 364, 380) sts. Work even for – (3, 3, 3, 1, 1) row(s).

BODY
ALL SIZES

Join Back and Front (RS): Work to 1 st after first marker, keeping marker in place, transfer next 53 (57, 61, 65, 69, 73) sts to waste yarn for Left Sleeve, CO 6 (8, 10, 12, 14, 20) sts for underarm, p1, sm, work 39 (43, 47, 51, 55, 57) sts, pm, work to 1 st after third marker, transfer next 53 (57, 61, 65, 69, 73) sts to waste yarn for Right Sleeve, CO 6 (8, 10, 12, 14, 20) sts for

underarm, work to end—174 (194, 214, 234, 254, 274) sts remain. Continuing to work in patterns as established, work even until piece measures 4" from underarm, or to 8" less than desired total length to bottom edge, ending with a WS row.

Pockets

Setup Row 1 (RS): Work 4 sts, [k1-f/b] 10 (10, 12, 12, 12, 12) times, work to last 14 (14, 16, 16, 16, 16) sts, [k1-f/b] 10 (10, 12, 12, 12, 12) times, work to end.

Setup Row 2a (WS): Work 4 sts, [slip 1 wyif, p1] 10 (10, 12, 12, 12, 12) times, work to last 24 (24, 28, 28, 28, 28) sts, [p1, slip 1 wyif] 10 (10, 12, 12, 12, 12) times, turn.

Setup Row 2b (RS): [K1, slip 1 wyif] 9 (9, 11, 11, 11, 11) times, k1, mark last st worked with safety pin, turn.

Setup Row 2c (WS): Slip 1 wyif, *slip 1 wyib, p1; repeat from * to last 4 sts, work to end.

Setup Row 3a (RS): Work 4 sts, [slip 1 wyib, k1] 10 (10, 12, 12, 12, 12) times, work to last 24 (24, 28, 28, 28, 28) sts, [k1, slip 1 wyib] 10 (10, 12, 12, 12, 12) times, turn.

Setup Row 3b (WS): [P1, slip 1 wyib] 9 (9, 11, 11, 11, 11) times, p1, mark last st worked with safety pin, turn.

Setup Row 3c (RS): Slip 1 wyib, *slip 1 wyif, k1; repeat from * to last 4 sts, work to end.

Row 1a (WS): Work 4 sts, *slip 1 wyif, p1; repeat from * to pinned st, slip pinned

❶ SHAPING AT TOP OF HOOD COMPLETED

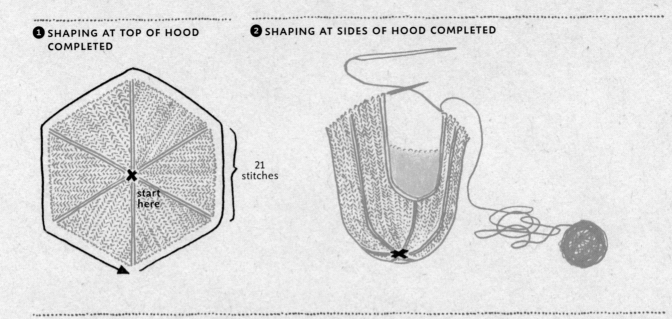

start here

21 stitches

❷ SHAPING AT SIDES OF HOOD COMPLETED

st wyif, work to next pinned st, **slip 1 wyif, p1; repeat from ** to last 5 sts, slip 1 wyif, turn.

Row 1b (RS): *K1, slip 1 wyif; repeat from * to 2 sts before pinned st, k1-f/b, slip 1 wyif, k1, move pin from st below to st just worked, bring yarn to front, change position of pinned st with st to its immediate left, keeping pinned st in front, slip 2 rearranged sts to left-hand needle, change position of last 2 sts on right-hand needle, keeping second st in front of first, transfer 2 rearranged sts from left-hand needle back to right-hand needle, turn.

Row 1c (WS): *P1, slip 1 wyib; repeat from * to last 5 sts, p1, work to end.

Row 2a (RS): Work 4 sts, *slip 1 wyib, k1; repeat from * to pinned st, slip pinned

st wyib, work to next pinned st, slip pinned st wyib, **k1, slip 1 wyib; repeat from ** to last 4 sts, turn.

Row 2b (WS): *P1, slip 1 wyib; repeat from * to 2 sts before pinned st, p1-f/b, slip 1 wyib, p1, move pin from st below to st just worked, bring yarn to back, change position of pinned st with st to its immediate left, keeping pinned st in back, slip 2 rearranged sts to left-hand needle, change position of last 2 sts on right-hand needle, keeping second st behind first, transfer 2 rearranged sts from left-hand needle back to right-hand needle, turn.

Row 2c (RS): Slip 1 wyib, *slip 1 wyif, k1; repeat from * to last 4 sts, work to end.

Repeat Rows 1 (a, b, and c) and 2 (a, b, and c) until you have 52 (52, 60, 60,

60, 60) sts for each pocket, counting both front and inside pocket sts, ending with Row 2c.

Bottom of Pockets

Note: You will now continue the Pocket without shaping, enclosing the Pocket within the fabric of the Body. In order to do this, you will work the outside sts for the right Pocket and the inside sts for the left Pocket (1a), then the outside sts for the left Pocket only (1b), then the inside sts (1c). On Rows 2 (a, b, and c), you will work as established across the left Pocket, then work the outside sts for the right Pocket (2a), then the inside sts (2b), then the outside sts (2c).

Row 1a (WS): Work 4 sts; *p1, slip 1 wyib; repeat from * through pinned st, work to next pinned st, **slip 1 wyif, p1; repeat from ** to last 4 sts; turn.

Row 1b (RS): *Slip 1 wyif, k1; repeat from * to pinned st, turn.

Row 1c (WS): *Slip 1 wyif, p1; repeat from * to last 4 sts, work to end.

Row 2a (RS): Work 4 sts; *slip 1 wyif, k1; repeat from * to pinned st, work to next pinned st; **k1, sl1 wyib; repeat from ** to last 4 sts, turn.

Row 2b (WS): *P1, slip 1 wyib; repeat from * to pinned st, turn.

Row 2c (RS): *K1, slip 1 wyib; repeat from * to last 4 sts, work to end.

Repeat Rows 1 (a, b, and c) and 2 (a, b, and c) until Pockets measure 6" from top edge, ending after completing Row 1c.

Rejoin Pockets (RS): Work 3 sts, [ssk] 26 (26, 30, 30, 30, 30) times, work to next pocket, [k2tog] 26 (26, 30, 30, 30, 30) times, work to end.

RIBBING

Next Row (WS): Slip 2, k2, [work in 1x1 Rib to 1 st before marker, k1, sm, k1] 5 times, work in Rib to last 4 sts, k2, p2. Work even for 2". BO all sts in pattern.

SLEEVES

Transfer Sleeve sts from waste yarn to larger circ needle or dpns. With RS facing, join yarn at center underarm, pick up and knit 4 (5, 6, 7, 8, 9) sts from sts CO for underarm, knit to end, pick up and knit 4 (5, 6, 7, 8, 9) sts—61 (67, 73, 79, 85, 91) sts. Join for working in the rnd; pm for beginning of rnd. Knit 17 (13, 9, 9, 9, 7) rnds.

Shape Sleeve

Decrease Rnd: Decrease 2 sts this rnd, every 18 (14, 10, 10, 10, 8) rnds 2 (2, 6, 4, 1, 9) time(s), then every 16 (12, 8, 8, 8, 6) rnds 2 (4, 3, 6, 10, 4) times, as follows: K2, ssk, knit to last 4 sts, k2tog, k2—51 (53, 53, 57, 61, 63) sts remain. Work even until piece measures 14½ (15, 15½, 16, 16½, 17)" from underarm, decrease 1 st on last rnd—50 (52, 52, 56, 60, 62) sts remain.

Next Rnd: Change to smaller needles and 1x1 Rib; work even for 2". BO all sts in pattern.

FINISHING

Block piece as desired. Using sewing needle and matching thread, sew zipper to fronts.

TUTORIALS

The trick of revolutionary knitting is all in getting started, and there are just two special skills you need to know in order to complete the projects in this book: knitting in the round, and casting on in the middle. In this chapter I've provided step-by-step tutorials for several methods of doing both of these: the Easy Circular, Figure Eight, and Disappearing Loop Cast-Ons, and knitting in the round using double-pointed needles or one or two circular needles.

EASY CIRCULAR CAST-ON

The Easy Circular Cast-On is a simple method for beginning your work in the center. You begin by creating a single stitch, then increase over and over into that stitch until you have the desired number of cast-on stitches. In developing this cast-on method, I was inspired by the Estonian star stitch, which uses multiple increases like this to create lacework and special textured stitches called nupps.

BEGIN WITH AN OVERHAND LOOP

Make an overhand loop (the first half of a tie-your-shoes knot) and slip it onto a double-pointed needle (dpn), making sure that the knot is at the bottom of the needle (see Fig. 1). The loop of the knot will be your first stitch.

FOR AN EVEN NUMBER OF STITCHES:

*Knit into the first stitch (the knot) (see Fig. 2), leaving it on the left-hand needle. Bring the yarn to the front, then purl into the same stitch (see Fig. 3 and 4), leaving it on the left-hand needle. Repeat from * until you have made the desired number of stitches (see Fig. 5), slipping the knot off the left-hand needle as you complete the final cast-on stitch.

FOR AN ODD NUMBER OF STITCHES:

Knit into the first stitch (the knot) (see Fig. 2), leaving it on the left-hand needle. *Bring the yarn to the front as if to purl (creating a yarnover), then knit the stitch again, leaving it on the left-hand needle, thus creating two additional stitches (see Fig. 7). Repeat from * until you have made the desired number of stitches (see Fig. 8), slipping the knot off the left-hand needle as you complete the final cast-on stitch.

FOR BOTH EVEN AND ODD:

Distribute the stitches over the desired number of needles and begin working. When finishing, gently tug the tail to snug the cast-on stitches together before weaving in the ends.

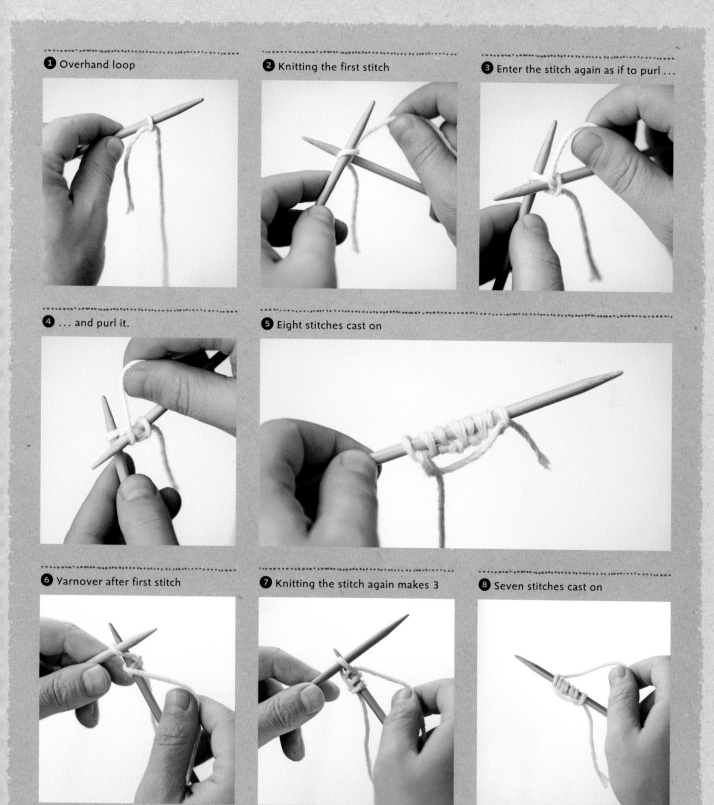

1 Overhand loop

2 Knitting the first stitch

3 Enter the stitch again as if to purl ...

4 ... and purl it.

5 Eight stitches cast on

6 Yarnover after first stitch

7 Knitting the stitch again makes 3

8 Seven stitches cast on

FIGURE EIGHT CAST-ON

This simple provisional cast-on creates a doubled line of stitches. Each upward-facing stitch is paired with a twin facing downward. In back-and-forth knitting, threading a loop of waste yarn through the downward-facing stitches will leave a line of live stitches at the ready for a nearly invisible join that may be used to continue knitting in the opposite direction. In center-out knitting, we will use both sides of our stitches right away. I find that this cast-on is easiest to work by using the Magic Loop Method (see page 152).

Hold both ends of a circular needle together with the points facing in the same direction.

Begin by placing the working yarn between the needles so the working yarn is going away from you and the tail hangs to the front (see Fig. 1).

Form a figure eight as follows:

Wrap the yarn over the top needle from back to front, and pass the yarn away from you between the needles, completing the top half of the figure eight (see Fig. 2).

Wrap the yarn under the bottom needle from back to front, and pass the yarn away from you between the needles, completing the bottom half of the figure eight (see Fig. 3).

Each figure eight will create one double-sided stitch. Continue forming figure eights until you have made the desired number of stitches (see Fig. 4 and 5). Before working the first round, be sure that each needle contains the same number of stitches.

Pull the end of the bottom needle to the right, sliding the stitches onto the cable of the needle, and freeing it to begin working the stitches by the Magic Loop Method. When completing the first round, work the upward-facing stitches normally (see Fig. 6 and 7). The downward-facing stitches will appear twisted—work these stitches through the back loops to untwist them.

The line of stitches created by the Figure Eight Cast-On will usually have a looser tension than the body of the work. You may wish to use needles one or two sizes smaller for the cast-on.

You may also adjust the tension after the cast-on has been completed and at least a few rounds of the pattern have been worked. Beginning with the final cast-on stitch and working backward toward the tail, gently tug the back (purl) side of the stitches to adjust to the desired tension. Finally, pull the tail to snug down the final stitch. The result (see Fig. 8) is a nearly invisible beginning.

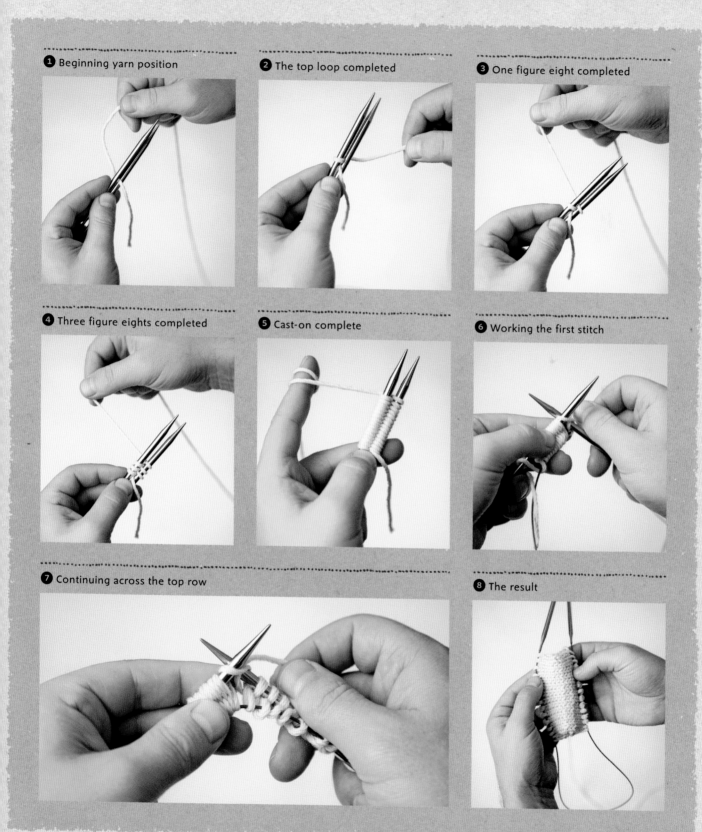

1 Beginning yarn position

2 The top loop completed

3 One figure eight completed

4 Three figure eights completed

5 Cast-on complete

6 Working the first stitch

7 Continuing across the top row

8 The result

DISAPPEARING LOOP CAST-ON

The Disappearing Loop Cast-On creates a tightly wrapped circle of stitches at the center of the work. It is used when a large number of stitches are needed at the beginning of a project. This method is also preferable when the yarn used is fragile or is not very bouncy.

This cast-on is nearly identical to the Figure Eight method (see page 146), except that the second needle used here is a five-inch-long weaving needle. You may use either a double-pointed needle (dpn) or circular needle as the working needle.

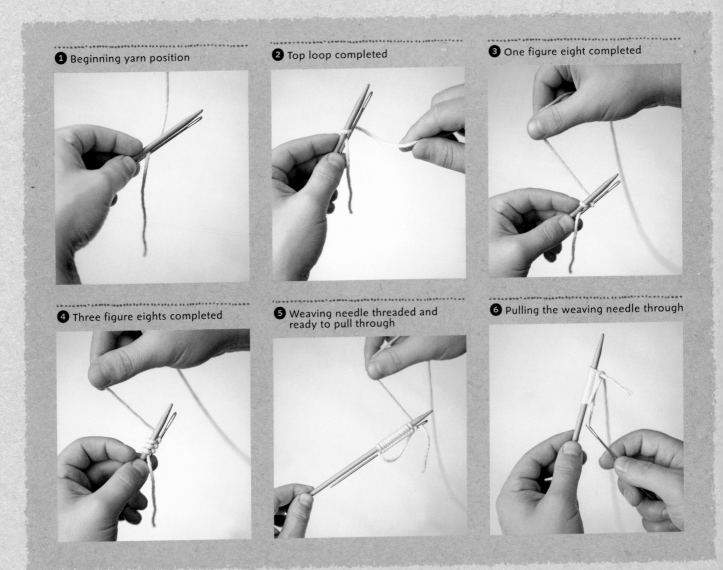

❶ Beginning yarn position

❷ Top loop completed

❸ One figure eight completed

❹ Three figure eights completed

❺ Weaving needle threaded and ready to pull through

❻ Pulling the weaving needle through

Hold a weaving needle below the working needle with the eye aligned with the tip of the working needle. Place the yarn between the needles so the working yarn is going away from you and the tail hangs to the front (see Fig. 1).

Form a figure eight between the working needle and weaving needle as follows:

Wrap the yarn over the top needle from back to front, and pass the yarn away from you between the needles, completing the top half of the figure eight (see Fig. 2).

Wrap the yarn under the weaving needle from back to front, and pass the yarn away from you between the needles, completing the bottom half of the figure eight (see Fig. 3).

Each figure eight will create one double-sided stitch. Continue forming figure eights (see Fig. 4) until you have made the desired number of stitches on the working needle. You will have one more stitch on the working needle than on the weaving needle.

Thread the tail through the eye of the weaving needle, then pull the needle through the stitches on the weaving needle (see Fig. 5 and 6).

Distribute the stitches over the desired number of needles and begin working (see below). When finishing, thread the tail through the center of the loops and pull tight before weaving in the ends (see below).

❶ Eight stitches divided among four dpns

❷ My right hand is holding the working yarn

❸ Working the first stitch

JOINING TO WORK IN THE ROUND

To begin a piece of center-out knitting, you first need to distribute your cast-on stitches into a circle. Forming this circle is what is meant by "join for working in the round." To begin working on double-pointed needles (dpn), distribute the cast-on stitches among multiple dpns and arrange the work into a circle so that the left-hand end of the final needle is just before the right-hand end of the first needle. If using the Easy Circular, Disappearing Loop, or Backward Loop cast-on methods, the working yarn will be to the left of the tail (see Fig. 1). Hold the working yarn (see Fig. 2) and begin working the stitches with an additional needle (see Fig. 3).

WORKING WITH DOUBLE-POINTED NEEDLES

I once brought an octagonal baby blanket to my local knitting circle. The pattern called for increases at eight even points, so to keep track of things I had divided my work among eight double-pointed needles. One more needle to work the stitches made nine. My friend said "that looks so complicated—how many needles are you using?" My immediate answer was "only two at a time."

Center-out knitting can look complicated, but no matter how we choose to divide our work, remember that we only ever use two needles at a time.

Just like in back-and-forth knitting, use the right-hand (working) needle to take stitches from the left-hand (holding) needle until the holding needle is empty (see Fig. 2 and 3). The emptied holding needle now becomes the working needle (see Fig. 4). Instead of turning the needles around and knitting back the way you came, continue working to the left. Take the next stitch from the right-hand end of the dpn to the left of the working yarn. This is continued from right to left around the needles.

Most knitters who have used metal dpns are familiar with the telltale "ting!" sound of a needle dropping out of their work and hitting the floor. Because needles with only a few stitches on them tend to slip out of the work, I recommend using dpns that grip the yarn and hold the stitches well. Bamboo, wood, and plastic needles generally work well and will easily stay put in the work, while aluminum and steel needles are much slipperier and are more likely to fall out of the work. Note that I used a metal needle in the photos for demonstration purposes.

❶ Center-out knitting in progress. The work is held on four needles.

❷ Using the steel working needle to complete the first stitch

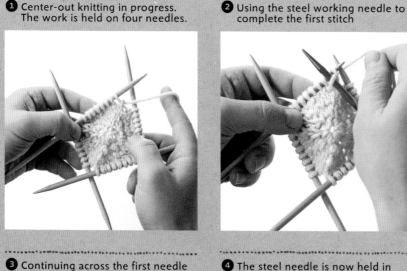

❸ Continuing across the first needle

❹ The steel needle is now held in place, and the first bamboo needle is freed to become the working needle.

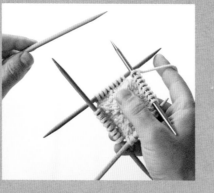

THE MAGIC LOOP METHOD

Instead of using double-pointed needles (dpns), many knitters find it preferable to work in the round using one long circular knitting needle. Choose a needle at least 36 inches long with a flexible cable and a smooth join between the cable and the needle.

To get started with the Magic Loop Method, divide your knitting into two sections, with about half of the stitches on each end of the circular needle. Hold the two needles parallel to each other with their points facing to the right (see page 142). *Note: The photo shows the work in progress.*

*Pull the end of the bottom needle to the right, sliding the stitches onto the cable of the needle and freeing it to work the top portion of the stitches (see Fig. 1). Use the free end of the needle to begin working across the top stitches (see Fig. 2). The cables will form loops on either side of the needles. Continue working across until the top needle has been emptied.

After the top needle has been emptied, pull the cable to the right to slide the bottom stitches into place on the needle. The two needles will now be held parallel to each other with their points facing to the left, and the cable hanging down behind them to the right. Rotate the work 180 degrees so that the needles are pointing to the right again and what had been the bottom needle is now the top needle (see Fig. 3). Repeat from *, rotating the work each time the top needle has been emptied.

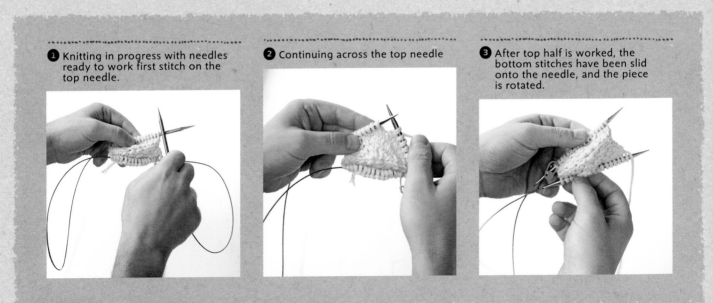

1 Knitting in progress with needles ready to work first stitch on the top needle.

2 Continuing across the top needle

3 After top half is worked, the bottom stitches have been slid onto the needle, and the piece is rotated.

As the work grows larger, you may find that you no longer have enough room on the needles to form two separate loops with the cable. When this happens, simply pull out the slack by pulling the cable out from the gap between two stitches wherever it is convenient. You may also find it easier to transfer the work from the long circular needle to a shorter circular needle when the piece has become large enough to fit on the shorter needle without stretching too much.

ALTERNATING BETWEEN TWO CIRCULAR NEEDLES

You may also alternate between two circular needles. Begin by arranging the stitches on the first circular needle as for the Magic Loop Method, then use the second needle to work the stitches (see Fig. 1 at right). Continue alternating between the two needles. This method can help you keep your place in your work. For example, many patterns contain a "resting round" every second round; if you alternate between two circular needles, every resting round will be worked with the same needle.

WORKING ONE CIRCULAR NEEDLE AND THEN ANOTHER

Using one circular needle and then another is a great technique when a pattern divides into two distinct sections, such as the top and bottom of a sock.

Begin by dividing the work, distributing the stitches between two circular needles (see Fig. 2 at right).

Slide the stitches into position on the first circular needle and work them with the free end of that same needle (see Fig. 3 at right). Once you have worked across the stitches on that needle, slide the stitches onto the cable of the needle. Turn the work and repeat the process with the second circular needle.

A NOTE FOR LEFT-TO-RIGHT KNITTERS

The instructions in the tutorials and patterns in this book are written for conventional right-to-left knitting. Since conventional knitting is worked to the left, conventional circular knitting is worked from right to left around the needles. Left-to-right circular knitting will be worked to the right. If you are already confident in adapting patterns to left-to-right knitting, remember that the shaping of each piece will also be mirrored. For example, a clockwise spiral motif written for right-to-left knitting would be rendered counter-clockwise if worked left-to-right..

❶ Bamboo needle taking up sts from steel needle

❷ Knitting in progress, divided between the red-cabled needle and clear-cabled needle

❸ Bamboo needle works stitches, red cable hangs down.

ADDITIONAL TECHNIQUES + ABBREVIATIONS

Backward Loop CO: Make a loop (using a slip knot) with the working yarn and place it on the right-hand needle (first st CO), *wind yarn around thumb clockwise, insert right-hand needle into the front of the loop on thumb, remove thumb and tighten st on needle; repeat from * for remaining sts to be CO, or for casting on at the end of a row in progress. *Note: When casting on a small number of sts at the beginning of a project, use the tail yarn rather than the working yarn to CO; this will give you a smoother beginning.*

BO: Bind off

Circ: Circular

CO: Cast on

Dpn: Double-pointed needle(s)

K: Knit

K1-f/b: Knit into the front loop and back loop of the same stitch to increase 1 stitch.

K1-tbl: Knit 1 stitch through the back loop.

K2tog: Knit 2 stitches together.

K3tog: Knit 3 stitches together.

Kitchener Stitch: Using a blunt tapestry needle, thread a length of yarn approximately 4 times the length of the section to be joined. Hold the pieces to be joined wrong sides together, with the needles holding the sts parallel, both ends pointing to the right. Working from right to left, insert tapestry needle into first st on front needle as if to purl, pull yarn through, leaving st on needle; insert tapestry needle into first st on back needle as if to knit, pull yarn through, leaving st on needle; *insert tapestry needle into first st on front needle as if to knit, pull yarn through, remove st from needle; insert tapestry needle into next st on front needle as if to purl, pull yarn through, leave st on needle; insert tapestry needle into first st on back needle as if to purl, pull yarn through, remove st from needle; insert tapestry needle into next st on back needle as if to knit, pull yarn through, leave st on needle.

Repeat from *, working 3 or 4 sts at a time, then go back and adjust tension to match the pieces being joined. When 1 st remains on each needle, cut yarn and pass through last 2 sts to fasten off.

Knitted CO: Make a loop (using a slip knot) with the working yarn and place it on the left-hand needle (first st CO), *knit into the st on the left-hand needle, draw up a loop but do not drop st from left-hand needle; place new loop on left-hand needle; repeat from * for remaining sts to be CO, or for casting on at the end of a row in progress.

LLI (left lifted increase): Pick up the stitch below the last stitch on the right-hand needle, picking up from the top down into the back of the stitch, and place on the left-hand needle; knit the picked-up stitch through the front loop to increase 1 stitch.

M1 or M1-l (make 1-left slanting): With the tip of the left-hand needle inserted from front to back, lift the strand between the 2 needles onto the left-hand needle; knit the strand through the back loop to increase 1 stitch.

M1-p (make 1 purlwise-right slanting): With the tip of the left-hand needle inserted from back to front, lift the strand between the 2 needles onto the left-hand needle; purl the strand through the front loop to increase 1 stitch.

M1-r (make 1-right slanting): With the tip of the left-hand needle inserted from back to front, lift the strand between the 2 needles onto the left-hand needle; knit the strand through the front loop to increase 1 stitch.

P1-f/b: Purl into the front loop and back loop of the same stitch to increase 1 stitch.

P2tog: Purl 2 stitches together.

Pm: Place marker

P: Purl

Psso (pass slipped stitch over): Pass the slipped stitch on the right-hand needle over the stitch(es) indicated in the instructions, as in binding off.

Rnd(s): Round(s)

RLI (right lifted increase): Pick up the stitch below the next stitch on the left-hand needle, picking up from the bottom up into the back of the stitch, and place it on the left-hand needle; knit the picked-up stitch through the front loop to increase 1 stitch.

RS: Right side

S2kp2: Slip the next 2 stitches together to the right-hand needle as if to knit 2 together, k1, pass the 2 slipped stitches over.

Short Row Shaping: Work the number of sts specified in the instructions, wrap and turn (wrp-t) as follows:

To wrap a knit st, bring yarn to the front (purl position), slip the next st purlwise to the right-hand needle, bring yarn to the back of work, return the slipped st on the right-hand needle to the left-hand needle purlwise; turn, ready to work the next row, leaving the remaining sts unworked. To wrap a purl stitch, work as for wrapping a knit st, but bring yarn to the back (knit position) before slipping the stitch, and to the front after slipping the stitch.

When short rows are completed, or when working progressively longer short rows, work the wrap together with the wrapped st as you come to it as follows:

If st is to be worked as a knit st, insert the right-hand needle into the wrap, from below, then into the wrapped st; k2tog; if st to be worked is a purl st, insert needle into the wrapped st, then down into the wrap; p2tog. (Wrap may be lifted onto the left-hand needle, then worked together with the wrapped st if this is easier.)

Skp (slip, knit, pass): Slip the next stitch knitwise to the right-hand needle, k1, pass the slipped stitch over the knit stitch.

Sm: Slip marker

Ssk (slip, slip, knit): Slip the next 2 stitches to the right-hand needle one at a time as if to knit; return them to the left-hand needle one at a time in their new orientation; knit them together through the back loops.

Sssk: Same as ssk, but worked on the next 3 stitches.

St(s): Stitch(es)

Tbl: Through the back loop

Tog: Together

WS: Wrong side

Wrp-t: Wrap and turn (see Short Row Shaping, this page)

Wyib: With yarn in back

Wyif: With yarn in front

Yo: Yarnover

RECOMMENDED READING

Vogue Knitting on the Go: Baby Blankets
Trisha Malcolm, ed.
(Sixth & Spring)

Mari Lynn Patrick's Octagonal Lace blanket published here is the pattern that sparked my fascination with revolutionary knitting.

Knitting Nature
Norah Gaughan
(STC Craft)

In *Knitting Nature*, Norah Gaughan used knitting to explore the beauty of science. Her book showed me how engaging and exciting knit design can be.

Symmetry: A Journey into the Patterns of Nature
Marcus du Sautoy
(Harper Perennial)

Du Sautoy's description of tromping around the Alhambra in search of examples of all seventeen types of symmetry is wonderfully engaging. Part history, part memoir, part mathematics, this book shares the excitement of discovery.

A Beginner's Guide to Constructing the Universe
Michael S. Schneider
(Harper Perennial)

The only book about math I've ever read in the bathtub. This book of mathematics is accessible, visual, hands-on, and suffused with magic and wonder.

First Book of Modern Lace Knitting
Second Book of Modern Lace Knitting
Marianne Kinzel
(Dover)

Knitted Lace Designs of Herbert Niebling
Eva Maria Leszner
(Lacis)

Marianne Kinzel and Herbert Niebling were both absolute masters of revolutionary knitting. Kinzel's work is symmetrical, beautiful, and precise, while the knitted lace doilies of Herbert Niebling are downright exuberant.

YARN SOURCES

If you can't find the yarns I used at your favorite retailer, contact the manufacturers and distributors below.

Alisha Goes Around
www.alishagoesaround.com

Blue Sky Alpacas
www.blueskyalpacas.com

Brooklyn Tweed Shelter
www.brooklyntweed.net

Brown Sheep
www.brownsheep.com

Crystal Palace Yarns
www.crystalpalaceyarns.com

The Fibre Company
Distributed by Kelbourne Woolens
www.kelbournewoolens.com

Green Mountain Spinnery
www.spinnery.com

Louet North America
www.louet.com

Madelinetosh
www.madelinetosh.com

Malabrigo
www.malabrigoyarn.com

Morehouse Merino
www.morehousefarm.com

O-Wool
www.o-wool.com

ShiBui Knits
www.shibuiknits.com

Skacel Collection, Inc.
www.skacelknitting.com

Solitude Wool
www.solitudewool.com

Spud & Chloe
www.spudandchloe.com

Swans Island Yarn
www.swansislandblankets.com

Verdant Gryphon
www.verdantgryphon.com

Woodstock Knits
www.woodstockknits.com

ACKNOWLEDGMENTS

This book is the work of many hands. Thank you to Susan J. Aitel, Tiger Buchman, D. BryAnn Chen, Pat Chen, Shameka Clarke, Papatya Curtis, Sandy Halpin, Margaux Hufnagel, Pony Knowles, Emilia Rosa, and Barbara Vaccarro, each of whom lent their considerable talents to knitting the projects. I've been blessed to be part of a vibrant, bicoastal community of fiber folk—thank you to the Men's Group at Knitty City and the entire Park Slope Knitting Circle, and to my local yarn shops, Downtown Yarns, Knitty City, and La Casita in NYC, and KnitPurl and Twisted in PDX.

I'd like to thank those whose work has inspired me to create this work: Katherine Cobey, Norah Gaughan, Bill Huntington, Paul Jackson, Chris Palmer, Michael Schneider, Radmila Vucovic, and Anna Zilboorg; and those who have encouraged me on this path, sometimes believing in me before I did: Teva Durham, Kristin Ford, Barbara Grossman, Meghan Kelley, Faye Saxton, Vicki Stiefel, and Bruce Weinstein. Thank you to my friends Scott Bodenner, Shana Norberg, and Bria Phillips for their feedback, suggestions, and encouragement as the book took shape.

Thank you to everyone involved in the production of this book: to my editor, Melanie Falick, for believing in the project, keeping me on track, and always encouraging me to dream bigger. Technical editor Sue McCain wrangled my often unorthodox designs into shape with patience, expertise, and good humor.

Thanks also to secondary technical editor Robin Melanson, who focused an additional pair of eagle eyes on the pattern instructions. Photographer Jody Rogac and stylist Karen Schaupeter made the garments come alive, Sun Young Park transformed my rough sketches into the accessible illustrations you see on so many of these pages, and designer Anna Christian combined all of these disparate elements into a pleasing whole. Thank you all.

Finally, I'd like to thank my parents for their constant love and support. And last and most of all to Sascha, for sticking by me throughout it all, always reminding me that it's magic and love that make the art go.

ABOUT THE AUTHOR

DANIEL YUHAS's work has been featured in the magazines *Interweave Knits*, *Knit.Wear*, *YarnForward*, and *Creative Knitting*; the Fresh Designs series of books, the books *The 10 Secrets of the LaidBack Knitters*, *Me Make Monster*, and *Luxury Yarn One-Skein Wonders*; and online on Knitty and KnitCircus. He lives in Portland, Oregon, and teaches nationwide. You can see what he's up to at www.revolutionaryknitting.com.